OA

BRISTOL CITY COUNCIL
BRISTOL LIBRARIES

S

THIS BOOK IS FOR USE
IN THE LIBRARY ONLY

 York Press

Nicola Alper is hereby identified as author of this work in accordance with
Section 77 of the Copyright, Designs and Patents Act 1988

The author would like to thank The Theatre Museum in Covent Garden for their
research facilities, Alan Ayckbourn and The Stephen Joseph Theatre.

YORK PRESS
322 Old Brompton Road, London SW5 9JH

PEARSON EDUCATION LIMITED
Edinburgh Gate, Harlow,
Essex CM20 2JE, United Kingdom
Associated companies, branches and representatives throughout the world

First published 1999

ISBN 0–582–38230–0

Designed by Vicki Pacey, Trojan Horse, London
Illustrated by Sue Scott
Phototypeset by Gem Graphics, Trenance, Mawgan Porth, Cornwall
Colour reproduction and film output by Spectrum Colour
Produced by Addison Wesley Longman China Limited, Hong Kong

CONTENTS

PREFACE

York Notes are designed to give you a broader perspective on works of literature studied at GCSE and equivalent levels. We have carried out extensive research into the needs of the modern literature student prior to publishing this new edition. Our research showed that no existing series fully met students' requirements. Rather than present a single authoritative approach, we have provided alternative viewpoints, empowering students to reach their own interpretations of the text. York Notes provide a close examination of the work and include biographical and historical background, summaries, glossaries, analyses of characters, themes, structure and language, cultural connections and literary terms.

If you look at the Contents page you will see the structure for the series. However, there's no need to read from the beginning to the end as you would with a novel, play, poem or short story. Use the Notes in the way that suits you. Our aim is to help you with your understanding of the work, not to dictate how you should learn.

York Notes are written by English teachers and examiners, with an expert knowledge of the subject. They show you how to succeed in coursework and examination assignments, guiding you through the text and offering practical advice. Questions and comments will extend, test and reinforce your knowledge. Attractive colour design and illustrations improve clarity and understanding, making these Notes easy to use and handy for quick reference.

York Notes are ideal for:
- Essay writing
- Exam preparation
- Class discussion

The author of these Notes is Nicky Alper, BA, PGCE, a coursework moderator and examiner for a major GCSE examination board, who has also published Notes on Hardy's *Far from the Madding Crowd*. She teaches English at a leading girls' independent school in Dorset.

The text used in these Notes is the Longman Literature Edition, editor Jacqueline Fisher (1977).

Health Warning: **This study guide will enhance your understanding, but should not replace the reading of the original text and/or study in class.**

PART ONE

INTRODUCTION

HOW TO STUDY A PLAY

You have bought this book because you wanted to study a play on your own. This may supplement classwork.

- Drama is a special 'kind' of writing (the technical term is 'genre') because it needs a performance in the theatre to arrive at a full interpretation of its meaning. When reading a play you have to imagine how it should be performed; the words alone will not be sufficient. Think of gestures and movements.

- Drama is always about conflict of some sort (it may be below the surface). Identify the conflicts in the play and you will be close to identifying the large ideas or themes which bind all the parts together.

- Make careful notes on themes, characters, plot and any sub-plots of the play.

- Playwrights find non-realistic ways of allowing an audience to see into the minds and motives of their characters. The 'soliloquy', in which a character speaks directly to the audience, is one such device. Does the play you are studying have any such passages?

- Which characters do you like or dislike in the play? Why? Do your sympathies change as you see more of these characters?

- Think of the playwright writing the play. Why were these particular arrangements of events, these particular sets of characters and these particular speeches chosen?

Studying on your own requires self-discipline and a carefully thought-out work plan in order to be effective. Good luck.

ALAN AYCKBOURN'S BACKGROUND

Childhood

Alan Ayckbourn was born in 1939 in Hampstead, London. His father was leader of the London Symphony Orchestra; his mother was a journalist and writer of romantic fiction. His parents' first marriage did not work out, and at the age of seven, Ayckbourn found himself a boarder at a local school, when his mother embarked on a second marriage with a bank manager. At twelve he won a bank scholarship to Haileybury public school, where he had opportunities to act in Shakespeare's plays, touring abroad in the school holidays. He left school with A Levels in English and History.

Early career

Ayckbourn's first short job was as an ASM (assistant stage manager) at the Edinburgh Festival, after which he worked at Worthing Rep and Leatherhead as an ASM and actor. In 1957 he became stage manager at the new Stephen Joseph Theatre-in-the-round at Scarborough and that winter was invited to work as stage manager and actor at Oxford Playhouse. While there are always plenty of actors around, stage managers with mechanical expertise are rare and therefore greatly valued. For the next few years Ayckbourn worked at Scarborough in the summer and toured with the company during the winter.

First plays

In 1959 when Ayckbourn expressed dissatisfaction with the acting parts he was given, Joseph suggested that he write his own plays. His first attempts were *Square Cat*, a **farce** (see Literary Terms) with mistaken identities and *Love after All*. He married Christine Roland, an actress in the company, and by the age of nineteen had two sons. He and Christine later separated. In 1960 – the final year in which National Service was compulsory – he deliberately scored only two marks in an intelligence test, and wangled a swift discharge with a 'bad' knee, after promising to find an agent for the medical officer, an aspiring writer. 1n 1961 he wrote

Standing Room Only and in 1963 *Mr Whatnot,* which received bad critical notices when it transferred from Stoke to London. Then, in 1964 Ayckbourn became a radio producer for the BBC.

West End
successes

Between 1965 and 1969 Ayckbourn returned to directing plays at Scarborough in the summer as well as working for the BBC. Joseph commissioned *Relatively Speaking,* which transferred to the West End. Ayckbourn also wrote *Ernie's Incredible Hallucinations,* his first successful play for children.

In 1970 he became Director of Productions at Scarborough and wrote *The Story So Far.* This was followed by a string of plays which transferred successfully to London including *Absurd Person Singular*

Ayckbourn has
experimented with
a range of
different forms.

(1972), *The Norman Conquests* (1973), *Absent Friends* (1974, London 1975), and *Bedroom Farce* (1975). Ayckbourn experiments with time in *Absurd Person Singular* by setting the three Acts in Christmas Past, Present and Future; the three plays of *The Norman Conquests* actually occur simultaneously in different parts of a country house; he also uses three different bedrooms for the staging of *Bedroom Farce. Absent Friends* is unusual in its use of continuous time and action.

Director at
the National
Theatre

In 1986 Ayckbourn was invited to work at the National Theatre as a director. In 1987 he won awards for his National Theatre productions of *A View from the Bridge* and *A Small Family Business,* which he wrote and directed as well as directing his own play *Henceforward* at Scarborough; he was awarded a CBE, and in 1997 he was knighted.

Recent work

His most recent plays are *Things We Do for Love* and *Comic Potential.* Critics have remarked on the more sombre tone of Ayckbourn's later plays. Ayckbourn still lives in Scarborough, spending forty-eight weeks each year directing at the Stephen Joseph Theatre. His plays are written only a few weeks before the rehearsal deadline. He often thinks of the titles first. *Absent Friends*, for example, is a drinking toast: the play is a tea party with no alcohol. Ayckbourn begins writing at night in longhand. Then he dictates changes to his partner, Heather Stoney, who played Diana in the 1974 production of *Absent Friends* in Scarborough. *Absent Friends* was unusual, as Ayckbourn rewrote a scene between Colin and Paul during the rehearsal period (see Questions to Ayckbourn).

An amazingly prolific writer, he has written fifty-four stage plays, two television plays and collaborated on a film screenplay. His work is very popular; his plays have been translated into thirty languages and are performed throughout the world.

CONTEXT & SETTING

Stephen Joseph and Theatre-in-the-round

Seeing theatre-in-the-round in America inspired the director, Stephen Joseph to set up the first theatre-in-the-round in Scarborough in 1975. He employed Ayckbourn as a stage manager and an actor also commissioning his first play.

The traditional theatre has a proscenium arch with the audience facing the front in rows, sitting in the stalls, circle, gallery or plush boxes; productions involve expensive sets, costumes and lighting; the actors have to project their voices a long way; tickets are expensive to cover all the costs. Theatre therefore tends to be an elitist, middle-class pastime.

Stephen Joseph sought to popularise the theatre, making it accessible to a wider audience – like television and films. His theatre-in-the-round was designed like a boxing ring with seats on all sides; requiring no wings or scenery and few stage staff; ticket prices could therefore be kept low. The original theatre where

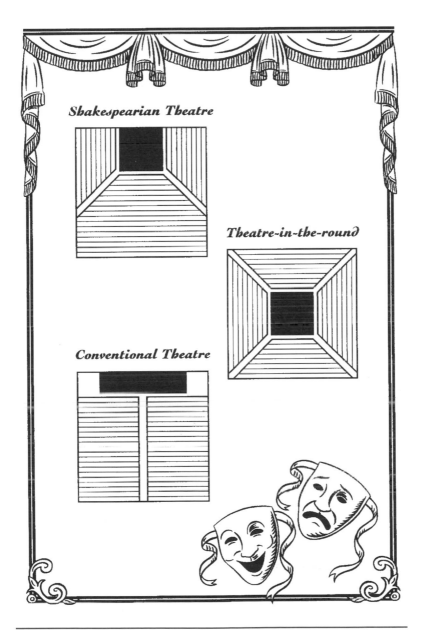

Shakespearian Theatre

Theatre-in-the-round

Conventional Theatre

bsent Friends was first performed had only 200 seats with two entrances for the actors. Because of the theatre's intimate size, the actors could speak more naturally and quietly, and the atmosphere was more appropriate to the domestic situations in his plays.

New Playwrights

Another advantage of low overheads was that Stephen Joseph could give new writers an opportunity to have their work performed, a risk that West End theatres are rarely willing to take. Ayckbourn has continued this tradition. In 1974 when *Absent Friends* was first performed there were ten plays, four of which were new. In 1998 Ayckbourn commissioned ten new plays for Scarborough. Ayckbourn directs his own plays when they are first performed.

Women and work in the 1970s

Ayckbourn writes about the new male entrepreneurial middle classes, which were encouraged by the Market Forces of Conservative governments (1970–74; 1979–97) – Paul is a successful example. Unlike his female contemporary Caryl Churchill, Ayckbourn does not reflect the great career opportunities enjoyed by modern women. Both playwrights show that the price of success entails ruthless, selfish behaviour in the characters' personal lives. In 1970 the Equal Pay Act required employers to provide equal pay for equal work and in 1975 the Sex Discrimination Act laid down guidelines on fair recruitment policies. However, a 'glass ceiling effect' is still in operation: the majority of women do not rise above middle management and many hold poorly paid part-time jobs like Evelyn.

Sexism prevails in domestic work too – both Marge and Diana shoulder the housework, cooking and nursing. As Ayckbourn says (see Questions), Paul would feel he had failed as provider if Diana had to work. However, part of Diana's dilemma arises from the fact she has no outside cultural interests or a career; her only function is as a housewife and hostess.

Divorce   In 1970 the divorce reform movement proposed a no-fault divorce when a marriage had 'irretrievably broken down', liberalising the divorce laws. Previously, divorce could only be obtained by proving adultery or cruelty or desertion. By the early 1980s the divorce rate was higher: one in three marriages ended in divorce.

Diana has grounds for divorce in Paul's adultery. She would probably be awarded custody of the children and maintenance, as Paul is often absent on business. However, women like Diana would have been brought up to believe that marriage was for life; witness her painful attention to the tips in Evelyn's magazine. By contrast Evelyn is from a younger generation and despises such advice: her husband 'can stuff it' (p. 12). Divorce was still a social stigma in the 1970s, so Diana prefers to remain married until forced by Colin to realise that her marriage is over.

QUESTIONS TO ALAN AYCKBOURN

In summer 1998, Alan Ayckbourn was busy directing at the Stephen Joseph Theatre; he agreed to answer the following questions sent to him by the author.

Why did you decide to choose continuous time and the same setting in both acts of *Absent Friends*?

A.A.   In every one of my plays I make a very early decision as to the time span the piece will cover. This, you'll understand, affects so many other decisions.

Were you disappointed that the play received such a mixed reception when it was first performed?

A.A.   Actually, the first Scarborough production got almost universally good reviews, both locally and from the nationals that covered it. The

London production (which I didn't direct) did get a much more lukewarm reception. But then I didn't care for it either. Significantly, it was one of the last shows of mine to go into London directed by someone other than myself. (I think there were two more, subsequently).

In the first draft you wrote a dialogue in Act II between Colin and Paul, which you later removed, using only Paul's 'manic uncontrollable laughter'. What was the dialogue about and why did you remove it?

A.A.   I can't remember the speech now. But I suspect that, like so many dramatists (including Chekhov, so I'm in good company), I found that once the play was 'on its feet' the actor could express twice as much by what he/she *didn't* say: the art of the unspoken.

Did you make any other significant changes to the text before performance or publication?

A.A.   Can't remember many.

Is the character Evelyn deliberately a 'trouble maker', consciously aware of the effect of her cynical remarks on Diana and Marge; or is she just morose, tactless and unintelligent? Can the actress choose which way to play her?

A.A.   Evelyn is from another generation. She despises the conventional female attitudes expressed by Diana and Marge. She is, if you like, an early example of the 'new' woman: one who didn't automatically go along with the subservient attitude to men. She's not stupid. She just has no interest in making an impression. She's short on social graces. It's probably a complete reaction to what she sees going on around her. I have a suspicion she's going to be a very good mother.

The 1970s were a time of great career opportunities for women, so why is it only Evelyn who has a part-time job?

A.A.   The 1970s were the turning point. Women were still divided into those who worked and those who didn't. Diana doesn't work because she is married to a man who would see her working as a sign of weakness: that he was unable to provide adequately for his family. Marge is largely housebound because of her invalid husband. She probably, again, has a part-time job; it's just never mentioned.

Do you think that Diana's life has been wasted 'doing all the wrong things' as she says?

A.A.   I think this was part of the 1970s' crossroads for women. Many of them were brought up by their mothers to believe that their responsibility was first and foremost to husband and family. I think they were only 'the wrong things' for Diana because they didn't work out. She'd have been perfectly happy to be a wife and a mother only she's not been allowed to pursue either function. Her children have been sent away and her husband is never there.

Most of the marriages in the play are unhappy. Do you see the destruction of romance and love as inevitable?

A.A.   Depends on your expectations. I think most marriages are doomed to be disappointing. The happy ones don't make very interesting theatre, either.

What do you think is the funniest moment in the play?

A.A. Couldn't say. Probably some of Colin's (well-meant) long speeches.

Did you intend the ending of the play to be predominantly hopeful or pessimistic?

A.A. It's an open ending. Love has finally died between Diana and Paul – or rather finally been declared dead. I think there hadn't been much life in it for some time but often we go on going through the motions of love, as if we still loved someone, because the truth is too painful. It takes a catalyst like Colin to force us to review our lives. On the other hand, life goes on. In the face of everything, we continue to live our lives and even look forward to tomorrow.

Have you ever met someone like Colin?

A.A. Yes. Several.

Do you think the play would be as relevant today if it were to be revived? Would you like to see it performed again?

A.A. It has been revived, only last year. Here in Scarborough. I think a lot of it is still very relevant. Human nature doesn't change. We just adopt different hair styles.

PART TWO

Summaries

General summary

Act I
Part 1
(pages 1–29)
Before Colin's
arrival

It is three o'clock on a Saturday afternoon. Diana and her guest, Evelyn, are in the living room of her house, awaiting the arrival of Diana's husband Paul and the other guests. Diana has organised a tea party for Colin, an old friend, who lost his fiancée, Carol, in a tragic drowning accident two months ago. Diana makes a speech, hinting she suspects Evelyn is having an affair with her husband; Evelyn doesn't respond. Marge, Diana's old friend, arrives without her husband Gordon, whom she's left ill in bed at home. Marge admires Evelyn's baby and then seeks approval for her new shoes. She has bought Diana a small present.

When Evelyn leaves the room, Diana confides her jealous suspicions to Marge who listens and confides her own disappointment that she and Gordon can't have children. Marge telephones Gordon, who complains that he has hurt himself trying to find some nose drops. Evelyn reads a magazine, ignoring Diana until forced to speak. When Paul enters he commands attention, complaining about his poor squash opponent and pretending he's forgotten Colin and the tea party; Diana and Paul quarrel; Paul goes upstairs to work. Off stage Diana tries to persuade him to return.

Evelyn tells Marge she did have sex, once, with Paul – last Saturday – and later told her husband John. Marge is disgusted. John arrives; Evelyn nags him and mocks his useless cheap purchases. Diana reappears, clearly nervous, and snaps at John. Finally Paul comes in and criticises Diana for organising the tea party, insisting they can't comfort Colin. Diana and Paul quarrel; Marge acts as peacemaker. Diana openly accuses Paul of infidelity. At the height of their argument the telephone rings: Gordon has spilt cough medicine over himself and the bed. Then Evelyn's baby wakes up crying; she and John start arguing as she attempts to leave. At the climax of the chaos, the doorbell rings. Colin has arrived.

Act I
Part 2
(pages 29–41)
After Colin's
arrival

Evelyn retreats with the pram to the garden; Diana flees to the kitchen; Marge answers the door. Alone with John, Paul discovers that John hasn't told Diana about Evelyn. Marge returns with Colin, then leaves to look after Diana. The men seem pleased to see Colin, who asks for details about Evelyn, whom he has never met and the others' business affairs. Paul leaves to fetch Diana; Colin is alone with John.

All the characters return to the living room to greet Colin. Diana acts as hostess, pouring tea. They make polite small talk, until Colin raises the subject of Carol's death. Diana expresses their sympathy and is alarmed when Colin abruptly leaves the room. Paul deliberately tries to upset Diana, but Colin has only gone to fetch his photograph albums. Marge and Diana particularly admire the snaps. Colin then makes a long speech, describing his feeling about Carol's death and his pleasure at seeing his dear friends again, happily married. Diana exits in hysteria; the others are embarrassed and upset.

Act II
(pages 42–66)
Events leading
to Diana's
breakdown

It's now four-fifteen p.m.; time is continuous. Colin packs away the photographs and praises Diana to Paul, recalling he was once a rival suitor. When John goes out, Colin praises his character to Evelyn. Diana re-enters with the cream. After John returns, having checked his baby in the garden, Colin recalls their abortive excursion to a stately home: only he has happy memories of the day. Colin gives his views on the absent friend, Gordon. Then he tells the romantic story of Carol's first kiss. Paul is unable to prevent Colin relating that Paul once broke a china ornament at Diana's parents' house, hiding the pieces in his pocket at teatime. Even more embarrassing is Colin's narrative about Paul stealing Diana's table napkin. Paul deliberately hurts Diana by informing everyone that he now uses this table napkin to clean the car. Diana then pours the cream over his head.

Paul storms off upstairs, while Marge cleans up the mess. Colin makes matters worse by telling Diana that Paul is really gentle inside, advising her to love him. Diana makes a long speech about a disappointing childhood birthday present, a red coat that did not suit her; then expresses her sadness that she was not allowed to become a Mounted Policeman and that her life has been wasted. She becomes hysterical, screaming when Paul tries to touch her and swearing at Evelyn to leave. Diana only allows Marge and John to assist her upstairs. Colin voices his disquiet. Marge returns with the news Diana has been sick on the stairs; she orders Evelyn to clean it up. Colin stubbornly advises Paul to see Diana, whom he insists worships Paul, but Paul refuses, collapsing into crazy laughter. John returns; Marge has calmed and sedated Diana. Gordon rings again to complain about his burst hot-water bottle; both John and Colin eavesdrop. Colin even intervenes in their argument with well-intentioned advice.

Evelyn tells John it's time to go. Marge returns, as Diana is nearly asleep. She accepts Colin's apologies, but gets irritated by further advice. Colin finally leaves and the other characters collapse with exhaustion.

A<small>CT</small> I: <small>PART</small> 1

pages 1–29

The play starts at three p.m. on Saturday in the living room of an expensively furnished but tasteless 'modern executive-style house'. The table is laid for tea. Evelyn, a young woman, is chewing gum and singing while she rocks a pram. Diana the hostess enters and asks if the baby is asleep. She worries that the baby has too many covers, but Evelyn, the mother, is indifferent. Diana enquires whether John, Evelyn's husband, is coming. Diana complains about her husband Paul's obsession with squash. She is ill at ease, tensely awaiting the

Notice the ordinary setting and the tense atmosphere.

arrival of her husband Paul. Suddenly she launches into a **dramatic monologue** (see Literary Terms), revealing her insecurity about her marriage. Hinting that she suspects Evelyn is having an affair with Paul, she says that she would rather know the truth; she has discovered that Paul lied to her last Saturday to get out of the house.

The doorbell rings as Marge, another friend, arrives. Marge is childless and fusses over the baby, admiring him. There is some humour over the way she mistakes his commonplace name Wayne for the more romantic Walter. Marge is anxious to have her new shoes admired, although worried about her husband Gordon, who is ill in bed at home. She has bought Diana a present, a kitchen towel-holder, which Diana insists on paying for despite Marge's protests. Evelyn leaves the room to go to the lavatory.

Alone, the two women confide their concerns. Diana seeks sympathy for her jealous suspicions about her husband Paul, having an affair with Evelyn. She cites Paul's reluctance to invite Evelyn and John this afternoon as well as his strange behaviour, washing a shirt in the middle of the night as proof. She accuses Evelyn of snooping upstairs now and stealing a scarf. She is also unhappy that Paul has sent both their children away to boarding school. Marge attempts diversion by admiring Evelyn's baby, but Diana suggests that the baby's eyes are abnormal and complains that Paul never lets their daughter wear her glasses. Marge is sad because Gordon is against adoption, preferring to continue infertility tests. Feeling guilty she asks permission to ring Gordon.

Notice the tension generated by Marge and Gordon's telephone conversations throughout the play.

Evelyn returns to immerse herself in a magazine, although she too is forced insincerely to admire Marge's new shoes. Marge's telephone conversation is comical: she directs Gordon to the chest of drawers to locate some nose drops and voices sympathy when he bangs himself on the way. We learn that Gordon is large, overweight and accident-prone. Diana pointedly talks to Evelyn who is still ignoring them as she continues to chew gum and read her magazine.

Ayckbourn now reveals the reason for the gathering to the audience.

Diana and Marge discuss the purpose of this tea party: the friends are assembling to comfort Colin, whose fiancée, Carol recently drowned in a tragic accident at sea. They have not seen Colin for three years, as he had to relocate for his job. Both women think that Colin was close to their respective husbands. To ease Colin's embarrassment Diana has invited other friends too.

BEFORE COLIN'S ARRIVAL continued

Diana again addresses Evelyn, asking her what she is reading. Forced to respond Evelyn quotes some tips to keep husbands happy, from her woman's magazine. Diana listens anxiously, still believing she can prevent Paul from being unfaithful. There is humour in the contrast between Marge's and Diana's gullible and avid interest in traditional methods to keep your man and Evelyn's cynicism. Marge muses on the sad drowning of Carol only two months ago, but Diana sensibly reminds her that the main purpose of the tea party is to 'cheer Colin up' (p. 12).

Note the way that Paul dominates the room.

Paul, Diana's husband enters wearing a tracksuit, demanding that Diana find his shoes. He greets the women cursorily, making a silly joke about the baby. Again there is a contrast between Marge's and Diana's rapt attention to Paul and Evelyn's indifference; she momentarily lifts her eyes from her magazine. There is mystery: is this genuine rudeness or guilty embarrassment, because she is having an affair with Paul?

Paul hogs the limelight, complaining about his poor squash opponent and boasting about winning. Evelyn is deliberately rude, making a sarcastic comment while avoiding eye contact. Paul repeats his request that Diana locates his shoes and asks after Gordon. He makes rude comments about Gordon's prolonged ill health, then abruptly tries to leave, claiming he has work to do upstairs despite Diana's protests. He has to be reminded by Diana about the tea party and who Colin is. The audience must start to question whether Paul and Colin were ever good friends, as Diana has asserted. Paul and Diana disagree openly about whether she told him that Colin was coming. Diana made the arrangements two weeks ago. The conflict creates tension and reveals clearly to the audience that Paul rarely listens to Diana, but always takes note of business conversations. When Marge tactfully suggests that Paul may have forgotten, he becomes so aggressive that Diana intervenes. Paul retreats upstairs, ignoring Diana's protests and leaving her upset. Diana confides to Marge that Paul has done this before. She runs away to the kitchen. Her loss of control is **prophetically ironic** (see Literary Terms), preparing the audience for her breakdown in Act II. Evelyn appears to enjoy Diana's discomfort.

Ayckbourn confirms that Diana's instincts were right.

Marge and Evelyn are left alone on stage for the first time. Marge questions Evelyn about Paul, but Evelyn takes advantage of Marge's embarrassment by being deliberately obtuse. She only puts down her magazine reluctantly at Marge's direct request. When challenged directly about a 'love affair' (p. 16) she denies it, crudely stating that all that took place was a single loveless sexual act in the back of Paul's car. There is mystery: is she being crude to shock the disgusted Marge or because she is protesting at being used as a sexual object to further her husband's business plans? Her husband John relies on the successful Paul for favours in business. Certainly she made it plain to Paul afterwards that the sex was unpleasant, as he was very sweaty after a game of squash. Evelyn speaks dismissively of her own husband John's sexual prowess and disparages men. She reacts to Marge's disgust by terminating the conversation, burying herself in her magazine. Marge confides her revulsion at Evelyn's heartlessness to the innocent baby. Evelyn retaliates, making bitchy remarks about Marge's poor quality and unfashionable shoes.

Note the gradual rise in tension as another character arrives.

The doorbell ringing precipitates the first real action. While Marge vacillates about answering the door, Diana rushes in, panicking that Colin has arrived early. She answers the door and then disappears again. It's John, Evelyn's husband. She nags him for being late.

When John shows paternal interest in his baby son,
Evelyn worries that he will wake the baby. John and
Evelyn have a small tiff about whether the baby should
be kept awake during the day. He makes suggestive
sexual remarks about Diana's disappearance upstairs
with Paul – a touch of **dramatic irony** (see Literary
Terms), for the audience knows that Diana and Paul
are upstairs arguing. Marge shows up John's poor
judgement by pointedly glaring at Evelyn, who has
contributed to this marital discord. John like Paul is
keen to get the tea party over, again calling into
question whether he was really Colin's friend. John feels
uneasy about death, so Evelyn mocks him by repeating
the word. Marge starts to knit and John harps on about
sex as the explanation for his hosts' non-appearance.
His fidgety, restless movement adds to the tension. He
crows to Evelyn over his latest bargains: a fuel gauge
with a loose wire, a wing mirror with a missing screw
and some free carpet for the car. However, she is
unimpressed, pessimistically prophesying that the carpet
won't fit and citing previous so-called bargains such as a
vacuum cleaner with the wrong attachments, held on by
elastic bands and a mixer with the wrong bowl that
throws food onto the wall. Evelyn's wit reveals her
dissatisfaction and exasperation with her husband.
When John playfully mimes shadow boxing we feel that
he would really like to hit her.

*Ayckbourn
intermixes
humour with
tension.*

Diana finally reappears, having failed to persuade Paul
to come downstairs to meet Colin. She too doubts
whether Colin is Paul's 'best friend' (p. 21). John re-
echoes Diana's unease about their ability to cope with
Colin's grief without Paul's presence. Diana takes
refuge in small talk, by asking what Marge is knitting
and admiring the colour of the wool. Marge is making
a jumper for Gordon to protect his weak chest in the
wind. Then John enquires about Gordon: like Paul he

is impatient with Gordon's continual ill health. It is
humorous when John cites food poisoning as the cause,
and Marge informs him that Gordon now has another
different complaint. We are left feeling that Gordon is
a tiresome hypochondriac, who makes excessive
demands on the long-suffering Marge. Diana reveals
her closely controlled near-hysteria when she repeatedly
and politely asks John to sit down: he is clearly getting
on her nerves with his persistent pacing. Her shrill
remark about going 'mad' (p. 22) is **prophetically
ironic** (see Literary Terms). Both Diana and John vie
to apologise. Evelyn contributes to the tension by
sarcastically commenting on John's inability to sit down
at meal times.

They all sit in silence, trying to appear calm waiting for
either Paul or Colin to arrive. Diana is 'steeped in
worry' (p. 22), John attempts to keep still, while Marge
knits and only Evelyn is unconcerned, absorbed in her
magazine. Marge breaks the silence when she makes a
mistake with her knitting.

*Consider the
effect Paul's
reappearance has
on Diana.*

Finally Paul enters. He is perturbed by Diana's
apparent lack of concern and threatens to return
upstairs. John attempts to talk to Paul about a business
contract, but is firmly rebuffed. When Paul discovers
the kitchen towel-holder Marge bought for Diana, he
assumes Diana has made an unnecessary purchase, not
giving her a chance to explain. Paul questions the
purpose of this tea party, clearly at a loss to know what
to say to Colin, whom he hasn't seen for three years.
He doesn't believe they can comfort Colin. John
revoices his reluctance to discuss death. Both John and
Paul admit that they never liked Colin. However,
Diana reminds Paul that he and Colin used to be
inseparable, appearing regularly every weekend at her
house to see herself and her sister Barbara. Diana
deliberately tries to hurt Paul, claiming she and her

sister both 'fancied' (p. 24) Colin. When Marge and
Evelyn laugh, Diana pretends she was only joking.
Marge, the peacemaker, tries to stop Paul and Diana
bickering about the past by reminding them that their
purpose is to support Colin as friends. Evelyn mocks a
romantic love story in her magazine about a man's
ecstatic reaction to his girlfriend's kiss. This is
prophetically ironic (see Literary Terms): later in Act
II (p. 49) Colin recalls a similar reaction the first time
he kissed Carol. Diana and Paul resume their
argument: Diana asks Paul why he didn't court Barbara
instead if he really preferred her. When she virtually
accuses him of infidelity, Paul feigns incomprehension.
Marge again tries to stop the quarrel by suggesting a
cup of tea.

*Examine the way
Ayckbourn speeds
up the pace and
action.*

To add to the nervous tension the telephone starts to
ring and is ignored by the characters, while Marge
literally tries to part Diana and Paul. Paul embarrasses
Diana in front of the others, as she is reluctant to be
explicit about sex. At bay, Diana points at Evelyn as the
cause, who also feigns stupidity. Paul attempts to
defend Evelyn. Eventually John answers the telephone:
it's Gordon, who has had a domestic disaster, spilling
cough medicine in the bed and over his pyjamas. The
comedy becomes **farcical** and **ironic** (see Literary
Terms), as Marge's overreaction about stains on the
mattress and Gordon's pyjamas is counterpointed by
the serious destructive wrangling of Paul and Diana,
who are quarrelling about the sexual stains of infidelity.
Evelyn tries to leave, but is stopped by Paul demanding
that Diana provide proof. John too tries to stop Evelyn
leaving, citing Colin. In fact, he is worried about
upsetting Paul, a potential source of business. When
Paul attempts to touch Diana, she recoils hysterically.
At this dramatic point the baby wakes and cries,
provoking yet another argument as Evelyn blames John

and declares she is leaving. There are then three alterations occurring simultaneously.

Notice the way Colin's arrival is preceded by domestic chaos.

The climax is reached when the doorbell rings, heralding the arrival of Colin and blocking Evelyn's exit. There is black humour when Diana screams at Evelyn to leave and Evelyn replies 'I'm trying to' (p. 27). She is forced to retreat with the pram into the garden. Marge is so obsessed by the problem of stain removal that she is oblivious to Diana's distress. Nevertheless, Paul judges Marge to be the calmest and fittest person to answer the door. Diana has fled to the kitchen, unable to cope.

The two men, John and Paul are left alone for the first time. Paul asks John if he was responsible for informing Diana about Evelyn. In fact John was only too anxious to forget his wife's infidelity; believing a fuss would jeopardise his business relationship with Paul, easily reassured by Paul that it wouldn't happen again. Paul wonders whether Evelyn told Diana, but the mystery remains unsolved.

COMMENT

From the beginning of the play the audience senses the tension and strain in Diana.

Marge is the only childless female – her fussiness over Gordon, her baby substitute, on the telephone evokes **pathos** (see Literary Terms) as well as humour.

Humour is also created by the contrast between Evelyn's cynicism and Diana and Marge's efforts to please their husbands.

Notice the conflicting views of Colin – Ayckbourn creates mystery, as the audience awaits Colin's arrival.

Marge acts as peacemaker and is a loyal friend to Diana.

Diana's constant movements and irritability with both Paul and John reveal her rising stress levels and the deep malaise in her marriage.

Both comedy and tension are created by the three simultaneous arguments just before Colin arrives.

On Colin's arrival Diana again runs away which is **prophetically ironic** (see Literary Terms).

GLOSSARY

1 **cherubim** winged child angels with round faces, representing innocence

18 **Yellow Pages** a directory of business telephone numbers in alphabetical order

24 **the flower pot men** two similar puppets, Bill and Ben, characters in a popular children's television programme of the 1950s and 1960s

A *Identify the speaker.*

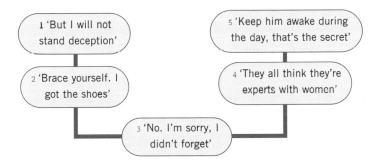

1 'But I will not stand deception'

2 'Brace yourself. I got the shoes'

3 'No. I'm sorry, I didn't forget'

4 'They all think they're experts with women'

5 'Keep him awake during the day, that's the secret'

Identify the person 'to whom' this comment refers.

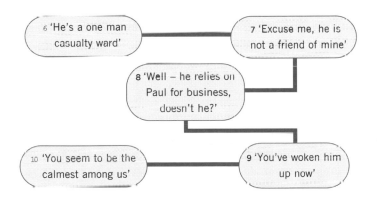

6 'He's a one man casualty ward'

7 'Excuse me, he is not a friend of mine'

8 'Well – he relies on Paul for business, doesn't he?'

9 'You've woken him up now'

10 'You seem to be the calmest among us'

Check your answers on page 74.

B *Consider these issues.*

a Think about why Ayckbourn begins the play with only Diana and Evelyn on stage.

b Consider how Diana and Paul's relationship is shown.

c Make notes on what the audience learns about Colin before he appears.

d Notice Marge's role as peacemaker.

pages 29–41

Ayckbourn makes Colin's entrance low key and friendly.

Marge enters with Colin. The two men appear pleased to see Colin their 'mate' (p. 29). Paul hugs Colin, while John shakes his hand. They make weak excuses for their absent wives. Colin is delighted that John is now a father, and reminds John that his ambition was always to have a son, while Gordon wanted to be a cricketer. He commiserates with Marge over Gordon's absence through illness and provides some literally sick humour by reminiscing about Gordon throwing up at his farewell party. This is **prophetically ironic** (see Literary Terms), as Diana later is sick on the stairs at this social gathering. Nevertheless, he manages rather tactlessly to upset Marge, who disappears to look after Diana in the kitchen.

The three men engage in polite conversation. Colin dutifully admires Paul's expensive modern house, while Paul acts as host, asking how Colin is feeling and offering him a cigar. He carelessly throws a cigar to John 'as an afterthought' (p. 30). The only small sign that Colin has suffered is his recent weight loss; otherwise he acts and speaks normally. John and Colin share a joke over the fact that they have both forgotten Evelyn's name; Colin asks for more details about Evelyn. Marge re-enters with some tea things, obviously embarrassed and beats a swift retreat with the excuse that Diana needs her handbag. Colin tries to remember the pet name the men all used for Marge in the past.

Note how the tension resumes and now involves Colin.

Finally Colin senses the tension in the house and asks if he has arrived too early. He wrongly assumes that John and Paul are still close friends. When John claims they do each other mutual favours in business, he is firmly put in his place by Paul, who makes sarcastic remarks about John's ineptitude as a salesman. Colin joins in Paul's cruel laughter at John's expense. Marge flits in briefly to get a comb for Diana; her angular form prompts Colin to recall her old nickname; the men laugh. Paul appears pleased to discover that Colin still has the same job in a bank, but makes an excuse to leave the room. There is mystery: is he really concerned enough about Diana and his marriage or does he merely want to save appearances, preserving the conventions in front of Colin?

John and Colin show their unease by their restless movements, pretending to admire Paul's expensive but tasteless pictures. Then John abruptly leaves for the kitchen and Colin is momentarily alone. There is suspense: what will happen next? Will Diana as hostess rally to the formal social occasion?

Ayckbourn uses all the characters to build to a climax at the end of Act I. All the characters, including Evelyn who was in the garden, return to the living room ostensibly united. Diana apologises and is kissed by Colin. John attempts to interest Paul in a business deal, talking figures, following him around the room, unaware that Paul is preoccupied and uninterested. Diana formally introduces Colin to Evelyn, who abruptly demands to know who has been talking about her to Colin. Diana even manages to make John sit down so they can all have tea; this looks like an ordinary innocuous social ritual. The characters assist Diana by also engaging in small talk, while she hands round the tea, remembering their preferences. Colin learns that Evelyn has a part-time job as a cashier. Marge mentions a mutual acquaintance she met in the street; John gamely assists her.

Ironically (see Literary Terms) Colin himself mentions the tragedy that has brought them together for the tea party, expressing regret that none of them ever met Carol. Diana attempts to articulate their sympathy and common humanity. Paul actively destroys the mood. Diana breaks off in embarrassment, after Colin thanks her. Colin suddenly rushes out of the room. There is

Notice how Paul tries to upset Diana.

confusion and mystery: has Colin run away like Diana because he can't cope or is there another less disturbing reason? Diana blames herself. While Marge reassures her, Paul picks yet another fight, blaming Diana for discussing the tragedy, rather than just trying to cheer Colin up. However, both Marge and Diana assert that it is better to express difficult emotions. John returns, having followed Colin outside to his car. Paul speculates that Colin has gone to fetch a rope to commit suicide, deliberately trying to upset Diana. Playing devil's advocate he claims that Colin's exterior cheerfulness masks despair, but both John and Diana disagree asserting that Colin's mood is cheerful. Paul rudely interrupts Marge when she rallies to the others' side. He urges them all to appear cheerful when Colin returns.

Colin returns, not with a suicide rope but with a photograph album and a large chocolate box containing loose photographs. The others are united in their visible relief. Colin sits on the sofa next to Diana ready to pass round photographs of Carol. He hands the most recent loose snaps of Carol and himself on holiday to Marge, while showing Diana the album. Both Diana and Marge express interest, admiring Carol's looks and her

Contrast the way characters react to Colin's photographs.

mother. The photographs are then passed to John, Paul and Evelyn: the descending order reflects their lack of sympathy and interest. There is a comic moment when Diana mistakes the back of the Natural History Museum for Carol's back garden. While Marge and Diana admire the people and the dog; Evelyn can only single out Carol's handbag! Diana bravely expresses amazement that Colin can bear to look at these photographs without becoming upset, but he reassures her, reminding them all of the universal nature of death and grief.

Act I concludes with Colin's **dramatic monologue** (see Literary Terms). Colin recalls the shock of Carol's sudden death by drowning. Yet he rejoices that such a 'perfect' (p. 40) person could love him and that he has such good friends: John, Paul, Diana and the absent Gordon. He is not envious of the others for being happily married. Colin's positive happy outlook and myopia provoke Diana to hysterical tears; she rushes off for the second time (preparing the audience for her total breakdown in Act II). Marge too starts to cry, John gives a forced weak smile and even Paul is speechless. Evelyn continues to chew moronically. Finally the obtuse Colin realises he has upset them.

COMMENT

Colin's obvious lack of tact creates humour from the start.

Notice the all male camaraderie as Paul and John greet Colin; the topics of conversation are less serious than when the women were alone earlier in Act I.

Diana acts bravely regaining control on stage while hosting an apparently conventional tea party.

Note the way each character reacts differently to Colin's talk about death.

Paul deliberately destroys the supportive atmosphere by picking a fight with Diana.

Colin's photographs reunite the characters, temporarily restoring a mood of normality.

Colin's final speech romanticises his friends' marriages, causing suffering to the characters on stage. There is **black humour** (see Literary Terms) in his myopia.

GLOSSARY   *40* **whooping** loud throaty noise, often preceding illness

A *Identify the speaker.*

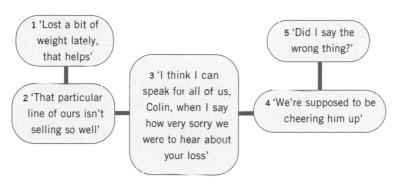

1 'Lost a bit of weight lately, that helps'

2 'That particular line of ours isn't selling so well'

3 'I think I can speak for all of us, Colin, when I say how very sorry we were to hear about your loss'

4 'We're supposed to be cheering him up'

5 'Did I say the wrong thing?'

Identify the person 'to whom' this comment refers.

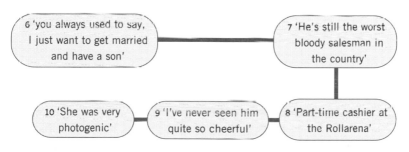

6 'you always used to say, I just want to get married and have a son'

7 'He's still the worst bloody salesman in the country'

8 'Part-time cashier at the Rollarena'

9 'I've never seen him quite so cheerful'

10 'She was very photogenic'

Check your answers on page 74.

B *Consider these issues.*

a Notice how Paul humiliates John in front of Colin.

b Contrast the way Marge supports Diana after Colin's arrival with Paul's behaviour.

c Examine the ways in which Ayckbourn builds to a climax at the end of this Act.

d Consider the effect Colin's final speech has on each of the characters.

EVENTS LEADING TO DIANA'S BREAKDOWN

pages 42–66   The curtain lifts. It's still the afternoon of the tea party, but now a quarter past four. Colin repeats his query as to whether he said anything wrong; the others lie awkwardly. Colin thinks the photographs upset Diana and starts to pack them away; the others help him. Colin theorises that Diana has been working too hard, pointing to the carefully prepared food as evidence. John is hungry, so he asks for a sandwich. Marge assists him in restoring normality by passing round the sandwiches and tells Colin that they would all like to see the photographs again later. Marge reassures Colin, saying that Diana is 'very sensitive' (p. 43). Colin tells Paul he is fortunate in his choice of wife. He recalls the past. At one time both he and Paul were courting Diana, claiming that it was fate that Diana preferred Paul, leaving Colin free to meet Carol later. When Colin voices his belief that Carol's spirit is still present, watching over him protectively, and talks about Carol's corpse, John is so upset that he leaves the room.

Then Colin praises the absent John to Evelyn, who questions Colin's judgements, feeling he has no experience with which to judge her marriage. Marge tries to stop Evelyn's cynicism. Paul deflects an argument by asking Colin how long he knew Carol. He too feels that with time their perfect romance would have ended, as Colin got to know Carol better by living with her. Colin is offended, so Paul backs off.

Notice how Ayckbourn prepares for the only real action in this Act: the pouring of the cream.   Diana enters carrying a jug of cream for the trifle, pretending that her prolonged absence was because she had to check the gas in the kitchen. She appears delighted that they have started to eat without her. Colin apologises to Diana for upsetting her. Diana makes barbed comments to Evelyn about John's superior caring skills: he is outside checking the baby.

Evelyn reads her magazine again, deliberately ignoring them.

Colin's well-meant advice to each of the characters creates humour. Colin attempts to calm the atmosphere by telling Evelyn that she looks depressed, and asking her if anything is wrong. **Ironically** (see Literary Terms) he claims that he has the 'knack' (p. 45) of judging character correctly by his first impressions. He states the obvious that she is worried about John but totally fails to perceive Evelyn's sarcasm: he advises her to appreciate John and be more giving. Evelyn stops Colin pontificating about Paul's character too.

John returns after checking his baby in the garden. Evelyn informs him that he has been the subject of conversation. They continue to eat sandwiches, until Colin reminds them of the last time they were all (except Evelyn) together. **Ironically** only he can recall the place. Everyone except Colin regards the expedition as a disaster: the stately home was closed; it poured with rain, Diana lost a glove and got soaked handing round the thermos for the picnic; Gordon drove too slowly and lost the others, while they all waited in a lay-by, and, finally, when they were reunited, they were overcharged at the tea place. The dialogue is humorous, especially Colin's sincerely repeated description of the day as 'marvellous' (p. 48) and his belief that Evelyn missed a great time.

Then Colin laments Gordon's absence, describing Gordon as big and shy. Paul and Diana bicker about whether Paul is big too. He praises Marge for her cooking, satisfying Gordon's large appetite. With Diana's and Marge's encouragement Colin relates the romantic story of his joy the first time Carol let him kiss her. Evelyn grunts cynically. We remember how Evelyn scoffed at a similar story in her woman's magazine.

Look at the skilful way Ayckbourn builds up to the cream jug incident.

Paul destroys the romantic mood by discussing football with Colin. It is significant that when Paul is asked whether he went to the match last Saturday, his reply is confused 'No. Yes' (p. 50). There is **dramatic irony** (see Literary Terms); the audience may recall that Paul used the match as an excuse last Saturday to leave the house and commit adultery with Evelyn in the back of his car. Diana urges the guests to eat more food. To Paul's dismay Marge offers to take any left-over food home for Gordon. Colin recalls other brilliant teas Diana made in the past, when he and Paul went to tea regularly every weekend. He annoys Paul by emphasising how strongly Paul admired Diana. Then despite Paul's protests he relates a comical and embarrassing anecdote: Paul broke a flying duck ornament and kept the pieces in his pocket, repairing it later. The other characters and the audience laugh at Paul here. Paul also stole Diana's table napkin as a keepsake – a romantic gesture, which delights Marge. Evelyn by contrast recalls how John roused her uncle's anger by stealing his screwdriver. Diana stops a squabble between Evelyn and John by offering more tea. Paul cruelly shatters any vestiges of romance when he informs everyone that he now uses Diana's napkin to clean the car, provoking the hurt Diana to pour the entire contents of the cream jug over his head. This moment is visually comic and also **pathetic** (see Literary Terms). The audience must feel that Paul deserves this. Ayckbourn has used **bathos** (see Literary Terms) to underline the erosion of romance through time in Diana and Paul's marriage.

Examine how Ayckbourn orchestrates the chaos after this dramatic incident.

Diana mouths a conventional apology, but leaves Marge to clear up. There is humour in Marge's overriding concern with the state of the furniture: the enraged Paul is left to stamp upstairs and clean himself up! Even the obtuse Colin is disconcerted. Diana returns to her

duties as hostess, offering yet more tea. Colin praises
Diana's tea and then launches into a marital advice
session. He feels Diana should be grateful for the
material success Paul has gained as well as her children,
exhorting her to love Paul despite his hard outward
appearance, which he believes conceals an inner
'gentleness' (p. 54). Colin's blindness and lack of
judgement must create uneasy laughter from the
audience. Evelyn asks Colin whether he writes for
magazines. Marge finishes cleaning up the chair. John's
conversation about cars with Colin is punctuated by
Evelyn's witty comments, implying that John buys
useless bargains.

Notice how
Ayckbourn shows
us Diana's
breakdown.

Diana is in a catatonic state, unable to respond with
praise to Marge's cleaning or even pour more tea. She
begins a **dramatic monologue** (see Literary Terms), a
childhood anecdote about her desire for a pretty red
coat in a shop window. Her mother bought Diana the
coat for her birthday, but Diana's delight was shattered
when she saw herself in the mirror and realised the
coat did not suit her. She had particularly wanted a
red coat, because this was the colour of the Canadian
Royal Mounted Police uniform. Her childhood
ambition had been to join the Mounties. However,

this was considered unsuitable for a girl, so she learned to type, married Paul and had children instead. She now regards her life as a failure and wishes she had joined the Mounties. Her hysterical breakdown is both **bathetic** (see Literary Terms) and also **pathetic** (see Literary Terms). We smile at her ambition to be a police officer in a handsome uniform and pity her despair. She sobs and then screams.

The polite tea party has erupted into domestic violence.

Marge acts swiftly, sending John to fetch Paul from upstairs; Evelyn just stares. Marge pushes Evelyn out of the way and starts to shake Diana. When Paul enters Marge orders him to get a doctor. Paul asks John to help him get Diana upstairs to bed, but Diana refuses to let Paul touch her. Marge fetches a cold cloth from the kitchen. Meanwhile Colin is useless in the crisis. Diana screams, swears and pushes Evelyn away, when she tries to help John lift her. Marge returns from the kitchen thrusting the wet flannel at Colin. She rejects John's suggestion that they slap Diana and persuades Diana to let them help her upstairs. Marge urges John to support Diana's weight more when he complains.

The aftermath, the dénouement or end of the play.

Colin, Paul and Evelyn relapse into shocked silence, broken by Paul's amazement at the cause of the hysteria. Colin finally expresses his opinion that

something is wrong, a long overdue remark provoking
uneasy laughter. Marge returns with the news that
Diana has been sick on the stairs, ordering Evelyn to
clean up the mess, as she is partly responsible for
Diana's distress. Surprisingly Evelyn obeys. Colin asks
Paul if there has been trouble like this before. He
advises Paul to go upstairs and see Diana; Paul sensibly
refuses. Evelyn returns from the kitchen armed with
paper towels. She feels depressed because the baby has
woken up and is crying.

*Colin tactlessly
gives Paul marital
advice.*

Left alone, Colin and Paul have an interesting dialogue:
Paul rudely interrupts Colin's nostalgic reminiscences
about the time when Carol had flu. Undeterred, Colin
persists in his view that Diana still loves Paul. He
recalls heart-to-heart chats with Diana when Paul was
going out with her sister Barbara. He regrets he didn't
know Carol long enough to develop the loving
relationship he believes Diana and Paul have. Thinking
he has cheered Paul up, he laughs. Only Paul's collapse
into crazy laughter alarms him. The humour here is
painful, nearly tragic. Evelyn returns and stares with
amazement at the men, declaring that she is going to
fetch her baby as it's raining. Paul finally stops laughing
and apologises to Colin.

John returns and the three men are together on stage.
He informs Paul that Marge has managed to give
Diana one of her sleeping tablets and will only phone
the doctor if the tablet fails to work. Paul thanks John
for his help. John assures Colin he is welcome to visit
his house where there is never a cross word: **ironically**
(see Literary Terms) implying the opposite by playfully
shadow boxing (a gesture used earlier in Act I – p. 21).
He eats more sandwiches. Colin hints he will depart
soon: Paul ignores him. John launches into a **dramatic
monologue** (see Literary Terms) with his mouth full,
not expecting anyone to listen, describing Evelyn, his

baby and himself as sharing a life of misery. He then
tries to interest Paul in his pet business proposition
again, Paul promises to think about the suggestion.

Note the effect of
the phone ringing
for the last time in
the play.

Gordon rings Marge for the second time. John
transfers the call to Marge upstairs, but instead of
replacing the receiver, he listens in, enjoying Gordon's
catalogue of domestic disasters: his hot-water bottle has
burst. Paul reminds John to respect their privacy and
forces him to replace the receiver. Colin expresses
regret, as he wanted to talk to Gordon. He recalls
Gordon's expertise as a left-arm bowler and his
unrealised ambition to play cricket for the county,
prevented by Gordon damaging his shoulder. Gordon
had to content himself with a career as a fire
prevention officer. John again lifts up the receiver,
ignoring Paul's ineffectual protests he laughs at
Gordon, who is ranting at Marge. This is surely very
black comedy (see Literary Terms)? The audience is
laughing at Marge's human misery – Gordon is a bully.
Colin unforgivably uses the telephone extension to give
unsolicited and badly timed marital advice to Gordon
and Marge. He fails to understand why Marge becomes
upset.

Evelyn returns pushing the pram, disregarding John's
request to leave the baby outside in the rain. Relieved
that the baby is nearly asleep, she discourages Colin
from cooing too loudly into the pram. Colin starts to
romanticise parenthood, but is rudely interrupted by
Evelyn. She tells John that it's time to leave. Colin
takes the hint and declares his intention of leaving as
soon as Marge reappears. John politely asks how Paul is
feeling. Paul says he will go upstairs soon as he has
work to do. Marge enters, reassuring them that Diana
is nearly asleep (like the baby). Colin agrees that sleep
will calm her down. Marge accepts Colin's apologies for
interrupting her telephone conversation, but she gets

annoyed when Colin presumes to advise her to cheer
Gordon up.

Ayckbourn employs The other characters collapse into exhausted silence;
an open ending, Colin finally takes the hint and decides it is time to go.
leaving the Marge kindly reminds him to take his photographs and
audience to think wishes him well. Colin reassures her: he visits Carol's
about the parents when he feels sad. John vaguely mentions that
characters' lives. he may visit Colin once he gets his new car. Paul
promises to give Colin's regards to Diana. Colin thanks
them all for their support, impervious to Marge's tactful
suggestion that with time he will get over Carol's death.
He smiles as he leaves.

Marge and John agree on Colin's essential niceness.
Paul politely refuses Marge's offer to return and help
him with Diana once she's seen to Gordon. Evelyn
sings to the baby, ignoring John's promise to fit the
new car carpet. The play ends with all the characters
except Marge silent, absorbed in their own concerns
and worries. Marge's **dramatic monologue** (see Literary
Terms) at the end shows that she is feeling guilty about
leaving Gordon, but is too tired to move. Her final
remark about the pleasure of spending time with good
friends resounds with hollow **irony** (see Literary
Terms).

COMMENT Diana's absence casts a pall over the mood at the start
of the Act.

Humour is created by the anecdote about the abortive
excursion to the stately home.

Ironically (see Literary Terms) Colin's memories show
a reversal in the balance of power: Paul was once a
humble suitor competing with Colin for Diana's
favour.

Notice how Diana pouring the cream over Paul is both
shocking and **farcical** (see Literary Terms).

Colin's ill-timed marital advice adds to the hysteria.

Diana's **dramatic monologue** (see Literary Terms) evokes **pathos** (see Literary Terms) and uneasy laughter – her childhood ambition seems ridiculous.

The comedy turns to tragedy fast: Diana breaks down and lashes out at Evelyn.

Marge copes superbly with the crisis; by contrast Colin is hopeless. John is surprisingly capable and supportive to Marge.

Colin's myopia becomes destructive. He contributes to the chaos: trying to reconcile Paul and Diana and fatally intervening in Marge and Gordon's telephone conversation.

Marge's final speech **ironically** (see Literary Terms) recalls the theme of friendship in the play.

GLOSSARY

44 **live wire** person with intense energy or alertness
46 **bee's knees** (cliché) person who is outstanding

A *Identify the speaker.*

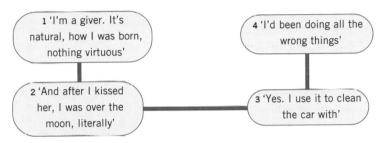

1 'I'm a giver. It's natural, how I was born, nothing virtuous'

2 'And after I kissed her, I was over the moon, literally'

3 'Yes. I use it to clean the car with'

4 'I'd been doing all the wrong things'

Identify the person 'to whom' this comment refers.

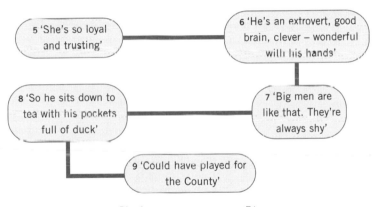

5 'She's so loyal and trusting'

6 'He's an extrovert, good brain, clever – wonderful with his hands'

7 'Big men are like that. They're always shy'

8 'So he sits down to tea with his pockets full of duck'

9 'Could have played for the County'

Check your answers on page 74.

B *Consider these issues.*

a Consider what we learn about Colin's relationship with Carol in this Act?

b Examine the humour created by the characters' different memories of the stately home excursion.

c Notice how Colin misjudges the characters of his friends.

d Think about the open ending of the play.

PART THREE

COMMENTARY

THEMES

LOVE AND MARRIAGE

Notice how Ayckbourn contrasts Colin's engagement with the others' marriages.

In *Absent Friends* love and marriage seem diametrically opposed. Colin's ideal love for Carol, his fiancée, **ironically** (see Literary Terms) survives, because she died young. Colin knew Carol for barely fifteen months. Paul sourly predicts that 'Time would have told' as Colin 'hadn't really time to get to know her' (p. 44), suggesting that with the familiarity of marriage love would have died.

All the marriages shown in the play are unhappy. Despite the romance of their courtship, when Paul was in awe of Diana's superior social status and had to compete with Colin for Diana, they have grown far apart over the twelve years of their marriage.

Diana came from a broken home: her mother left her father. This explains her insecurity and possessive jealousy; she wants to make her marriage work. However, Paul has been unfaithful several times and exploits John's dependence on him in business to have sex with Evelyn. He lies with ease and enjoys great freedom. When Diana breaks down; Paul shows very little concern.

Ironically (see Literary Terms) John's ambition was to marry and have a son, but Evelyn and John are having problems adjusting to their new baby. Evelyn is clearly dissatisfied with John's sexual and business performances, enraged at the way he wastes money on unsuitable bargains and complacently accepts her infidelities. She dominates him by sulking, being 'permanently unhappy' (p. 61). Like Paul she humiliates her partner publicly with destructive criticism.

ABSENT FRIENDS
Relationships

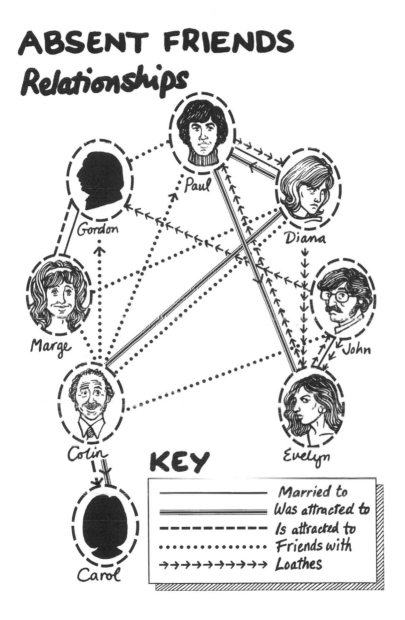

Paul

Gordon

Diana

Marge

John

Colin

Evelyn

Carol

KEY

————————	Married to
══════════	Was attracted to
– – – – – – – –	Is attracted to
••••••••••••••	Friends with
→→→→→→→→→	Loathes

Gordon controls Marge with his hypochondria, exploiting her guilt and caring nature. Although sterile he refuses to adopt. On the telephone he combines the roles of helpless baby and exacting spouse. Colin's idyllic memories are **juxtaposed** (see Literary Terms) to his friends' real problems.

FRIENDSHIP

Ayckbourn creates humour by contrasting the characters' opinions with Colin's.

The play's title **ironically** (see Literary Terms) echoes the **cliché** (see Literary Terms), 'Absence makes the heart grow fonder'. Although Colin left only three years ago, Paul barely remembers him; Marge only knew him 'slightly' as 'Gordon's friend really' (p. 10) – Gordon's illness makes him another absent friend; John never liked Colin; Evelyn never knew him. Memories are very subjective: while Paul regarded Colin as an unwelcome encumbrance, accompanying him on visits to Diana's parents, Colin has rosy views of their friendship. Colin values his childhood memories of 'Real Friends ... John and Paul and Gordon and Di' (p. 40). Indulging in nostalgia in the mistaken belief that he is pleasing his friends, he actually causes a great deal of pain.

Diana invites them all to this tea party because she has naïve faith in the healing powers of friendship to offer Colin vital sympathy and support in his loss, 'He'll need his friends' (p. 11). **Ironically** she declares the purpose of the gathering is to 'cheer Colin up' (p. 12); Colin actually plunges Diana into hysteria with the realisation that her marriage is over.

Marge is Diana's devoted friend.

Marge is a loyal supportive friend to Diana, generously giving small presents and sparing time from her onerous nursing duties to listen to Diana, who sadly admits she and Paul 'haven't talked for years' (p. 8). Acting as peacemaker, she braves Paul's wrath, leaping to Diana's defence. Sterling in a crisis, she instinctively knows how to calm the hysterical Diana.

At the end of the play Colin, undismayed by the chaos and suffering around him, declares he has found new 'good friends' (p. 65), in Carol's parents, a receptive audience for his memories. He invites them all back; only John vaguely responds.

Marge's final satisfied comment on the afternoon, 'Nice to sit with your friends now and again' (p. 66) is surely ironical

DEATH

Much of the conversation revolves around Colin's personal tragedy.

Diana seeks to help Colin over the awkwardness of discussing Carol's death – she died two months ago – by inviting his old friends. When Marge expresses her horror that Carol drowned, 'Poison, hanging shooting – that's never worried me but I'd hate to drown. You look so awful afterwards', Diana chides her for being 'morbid' (p. 12).

John is particularly squeamish about death, reacting sharply to Evelyn's teasing, 'Don't talk about it' (p. 19). He hastily finds an excuse to exit, when Colin mentions seeing Carol's corpse straight after the accident and his belief in ghosts, 'She can't communicate but she's watching me. Taking care of me' (p. 44).

Typically Paul is negative about the tea party, 'I can't see what good this is going to do for him'; Diana thinks it is 'natural to ask (Colin) around and comfort (him) a little' (p. 23). Paul is relieved that Colin only mentions his weight loss when asked 'How are you feeling?' (p. 30).

Notice how readily Colin speaks of Carol's death.

Colin himself brings up the topic of death, lamenting that his 'biggest regret is … none of you ever met Carol' (p. 35). Although 'upset at the time' (p. 39) he now gains happiness sharing his photographs and memories. Initially his final speech at the end of Act I is moving: he 'couldn't imagine' losing Carol, but when the fatal accident happened he wasn't there; he overcame his depression by consoling himself that he'd been loved by a 'perfect person' (p. 40). Colin happily relates his feelings after their first kiss 'I was singing and dancing and leaping over that common' (p. 49). We sense he is allowed licence to upset the others with his tactless well-meant remarks purely because they are embarrassed by his personal tragedy.

The play is also by implication about the death of Paul and Diana's marriage.

WORK

Refer to Context & Setting for more details on Women and Work.

Paul is dynamic and energetic, needing little sleep. He is a successful entrepreneur; rich enough to send both his children to boarding school and keep Diana idle, apart from tending their expensive modern house. His overdeveloped sense of competition and ruthlessness extend into other areas of his life: sport and sex.

John by contrast is far less successful with an eye for useless bargains, dependent on Paul for business favours. He needs to be woken every morning by his wife, who has to work part-time out of economic necessity. Colin has the same safe, steady job in banking, even though he relocated three years ago. Gordon, health permitting, works as a fire prevention officer. Evelyn is the only woman who works. She has a boring part-time job as cashier.

STRUCTURE

SETTING

In *Absent Friends* Ayckbourn observes the ancient Greek writer, Aristotle's idea of the **Dramatic Unities** of Time, Place and Action (see Literary Terms). The play has continuous action; the curtain falls briefly at the end of Act I, and all the action takes place in the

living room of Paul and Diana's house, creating a
claustrophobic, intense atmosphere. The open-plan
Scarborough Theatre-in-the round creates a feeling of
painful intimacy. The audience can easily imagine the
off-stage scenes upstairs: Paul and Diana's argument in
Act I and Marge nursing the hysterical Diana in Act II.

PLOT

Ayckbourn deliberately decided to avoid the **farce** (see
Literary Terms) of earlier plays. He wanted to get more
comedy from the characters and less from artificial,
improbable situations. In fact the characters' speeches
are far more important than the plot. The only obvious
comic theatrical **device** (see Literary Terms) – the
running gag of Marge and Gordon's telephone
conversations – is very plausible: Gordon is a possessive
husband resentful of time Marge spends away from
him. The superficially slapstick cream jug incident
again is both cleverly stage-managed and
psychologically truthful: the cream is meant to be for
the trifle and the audience has had earlier signs that
Diana is close to nervous collapse.

The reviews in 1974 were mixed. Many local critics at Scarborough in 1974 compared
Absent Friends unfavourably with earlier plays,
expressing the opinion that the play needed a faster
pace and the long speeches should be cut before it
transferred to the West End. Some London critics also
regarded the setting as too restrictive and the plot too
predictable, although others praised the play as moving,
and liked the disturbing open ending. In fact the long
speeches are one of the play's strengths, providing a
vehicle for social **satire** (see Literary Terms) on
middle-class suburban marriage and human weakness.
The pauses and awkward silences are both natural and
essential; the characters are embarrassed by having to
deal with the taboo subject of death.

USE OF SOUND

Ayckbourn skilfully exploits sound effects to create tension. Paul and Diana's argument rises to a crescendo as the phone rings, Marge deals with Gordon's complaints, Evelyn's baby starts crying and the doorbell rings heralding Colin's arrival. In Act II soon after Diana's breakdown the baby starts crying again. Colin's ill-judged remark, 'I don't know how you lot ever managed without me' (p. 60), is greeted by Paul's hysterical laughter. **Ironically** (see Literary Terms) Colin's cheerful bonhomie has wreaked havoc and destruction in his friend's marriage.

CHARACTERS

DIANA

Diana is in her late thirties, 'slightly fraught' with 'sharp, darting eyes' (p. 1). She knows Paul has been unfaithful on a number of occasions and her jealousy verges on paranoia. She has a social conscience, arranging the tea party to comfort Colin after his recent loss: **ironically** (see Literary Terms) Colin reduces her to hysteria. Placing friendship above jealousy, she invites Evelyn who she suspects is having an affair with Paul. Her **dramatic monologue** (see Literary Terms) reveals her low self-esteem. She admires Paul's cleverness and drive, although desperately claiming he 'needs' (p. 3) her.

Sensitive and caring

Faithful and jealous

Tense and neurotic

At ease with her friend Marge, she tactfully pretends she needs Marge's present and confides her jealous suspicions. She misses her children, Mark and Julie, whom Paul has sent to boarding school, and worries about their unhappy letters. Anxious to win Paul back, she believes the old-fashioned advice of women's magazines. Diana fails to stop Paul going upstairs to work, and rushes off crying to the kitchen. Off stage she fails to persuade Paul to come downstairs. Diana's nervous tension is revealed in her strident insistence that John sit down.

When Paul reappears they quarrel. Unlike Paul she articulates emotional needs, believing that as friends they can offer Colin support. Diana jokes that she and her sister both preferred Colin, deliberately upsetting Paul. They engage in mutual reproaches, asserting they married the wrong person. Diana voices her jealous suspicions, swearing at Evelyn to go, then screaming when Paul tries to touch her. She flees to the kitchen unable to cope when Colin arrives.

On her return she appears a capable hostess, but her composure is brittle. She listens sympathetically to Colin, sensitively trying to articulate their concern as fellow human beings. She worries when Colin suddenly exits, needing Marge's reassurance not Paul's destructive criticism. Her hysteria at the end of Act I prefigures her later breakdown.

Consider the way Ayckbourn shows Diana's psychological disintegration.

Diana's noticeable absence at the start of Act II casts a shadow until she re-enters to resume her duties as hostess. Her memories of the disastrous visit to the stately home evoke laughter. Typically she ran selflessly to each car in the rain offering hot drinks. Her remark 'there's nothing much can come between Paul and a football game' (p. 50) is **dramatically ironic** (see Literary Terms). She and the audience appreciate her sarcasm; Paul missed this particular football game to commit adultery with Evelyn.

She listens eagerly to Colin's account of the tea party at her parents' house, when Paul first visited, enjoying the romantic story of her missing table napkin. Wounded by Paul's public declaration that he now uses it to clean the car, she gets her revenge by pouring cream over Paul's head. Her speechlessness after Colin's advice to

'love' Paul 'for what he is' (p. 54) is ominous. In her
final **dramatic monologue** (see Literary Terms) she is
deeply depressed, regarding her life as a failure, even
though she renounced her ambition to join the
Mounties to serve Paul dutifully as a good wife and
mother to his children. She believes that she has 'been
doing all the wrong things' (p. 56); her frustrated
maternal feelings are particularly poignant. She breaks
down.

PAUL

*Successful and
ruthless
Arrogant
Unfaithful and
insensitive*

Paul's drive and ambition in business have made him
Diana's parents' social equal. His youthful awkwardness
and embarrassment, breaking the china duck, at
Diana's parents' tea party are a total contrast to his
self-important behaviour at Diana's tea party for Colin.

He arrives boasting that he beat his squash opponent.
'No competition. Lot of flabby old men' (p. 13). He
expects Diana to know where he mislaid his shoes and
jokes about Gordon's illnesses. Declaring he has work
upstairs, he humiliates Diana by pretending that she
never told him about Colin and the tea party. He
smugly claims that he 'never forgets things', because
he's 'trained' (p. 14) himself to run a successful business.
He ignores Diana by walking out – the pattern of
previous arguments. Evelyn suggests to Marge that Paul
is promiscuous. Off stage Paul and Diana argue.

Finally, when Paul re-emerges, he refuses to discuss
business with John and is rude about Marge's
superfluous gift. Insensitive, he can't understand how
they can help Colin. He becomes aggressive when
Diana jokes that she preferred Colin. After Diana
openly accuses him of infidelity, he brazens out the
situation, even blaming her for the breakdown of their
marriage 'how can a man live with a woman like that?'
(p. 27). He looks 'innocent' (p. 27), suggesting he is an
accomplished liar. Once Colin arrives, Paul urges Diana

to 'get a grip' on herself (p. 28). He accuses John of informing Diana about his sexual encounter with Evelyn; arrogantly assuming John won't make trouble as his business relies on Paul's favours.

By contrast he greets Colin affectionately. He asserts his superiority over John, the 'worst bloody salesman in the country', emphasising that favours are 'Generally one way' (p. 32). He repeatedly ignores John's attempts to discuss business matters and disrupts Diana's attempt to express their sympathy to Colin. Paul is a poor judge of mood, trying to make Diana feel guilty by describing Colin as 'On a knife edge' (p. 37); **ironically** (see Literary Terms) this accurately describes Diana. Paul is speechless when Colin envies his happy marriage. Typically, his only memories of the stately home visit are the 'waste of petrol' (p. 48) and the overpriced tea.

Notice Paul's mental cruelty to Diana.

He is embarrassed by Colin's questions about whether he attended the football match last week; the day of the adultery. Powerless to stop Colin's reminiscences, he feigns amnesia until the table napkin anecdote, then cruelly destroys the nostalgia by informing everyone he now uses it as a car rag. He reacts like a spoilt child when Diana pours cream over his head. His curse 'Bloody woman's off her head' (p. 53) is **prophetically ironic** (see Literary Terms). He storms off upstairs, only coming down again because John fetches him after Diana's breakdown. Paul leaves Marge to cope when Diana rejects him. He is insensitive, unable to comprehend why Diana is hysterical, despite admitting to Colin that there have been similar incidents. Paul refuses to see Diana and has difficulty restraining himself from speaking his mind to Colin, apologising only for laughing crazily.

Paul hints that the guests should leave by citing pressure of work rather than concern for his wife. At the end of the play he is snoring loudly, oblivious to the other characters' problems.

E VELYN

Morose and disillusioned

Cynical and critical

Consider whether there is any truth in John's description of Evelyn as a 'trouble maker' (p. 21).

Evelyn is directly contrasted to Diana with her negative outlook and lack of social skills. She wears heavy make-up, is young, quite fashionably dressed and 'expressionless' (p. 1). She is probably suffering from post-natal depression; irritable, mainly concerned to get her baby to sleep. She is taciturn, deliberately ignoring both Diana and Marge as she sits chewing gum and reading a magazine. She says nothing unless forced to. Unlike Diana she does not think her 'bloody husband' (p. 12) is worth pleasing and she mainly ignores Paul.

She is unashamed of the sex she had with Paul, rating even her husband John as a better performer. Cynical about men's sexual prowess, she admits that she is promiscuous. She seems hardened: John knows, but is indifferent. She deliberately shocks Marge, but is possibly protesting at being exploited as a sexual object in the male world of business.

She snaps at John for being late, mocking his fear of death. Exasperated by John's latest bargains, she predicts the free car carpet won't fit and criticises his other useless purchases. She exults that Diana will 'never get him to sit still' (p. 22) and sneers at a story about a man's delighted reaction to his sweetheart's first kiss. Acting dumb when Diana hints that she and Paul are having an affair, she tries to leave when Diana orders her out. When the baby wakes, she furiously blames John.

She works part-time as a cashier; certainly exhausted, combining care of a new baby with a boring job. She reacts impatiently to Colin's praise of John: far from him being a 'live-wire' (p. 44), she has to wake John every morning. When Diana praises John for tending

Evelyn mocks romantic love.

the baby in the garden, Evelyn reads her magazine, responding minimally in monosyllables. Colin exhorts Evelyn to be 'a giver' (p. 46) like himself; this is **dramatically ironic** (see Literary Terms) for she has slept with Paul and other available men. Later she grunts at the story of Colin and Carol's first kiss, also breaking the romantic mood with an anecdote about her uncle's wrath when John stole his screwdriver. She passively observes the mayhem, following the cream jug incident, staring curiously at the hysterical Diana, but makes no protest when ordered to clean up Diana's vomit.

John sees Evelyn as permanently depressed 'Misery is her natural state' (p. 61). She cheers up at the end of the play when she knows they are going, displaying maternal pride that her baby is fighting to stay awake and singing while she rocks the pram.

JOHN

Restless and unsuccessful

Insensitive and weak

John is a contrast to Paul; they are friends but not equals. John's dependence on Paul in business forces him to forgive Paul for sleeping with Evelyn and accept Paul's assurance it 'wouldn't happen again' (p. 28). As Evelyn bitterly remarks, John puts 'Business before pleasure' (p. 17).

He is a 'jigging, restless figure' (p. 18), irritating his wife, Evelyn, and the tense Diana. He shows paternal pride in his son, peering into the pram when he arrives and later checking the baby in the garden. He is reluctant to meet Colin, whom he has never liked. He makes sexual jokes about Diana and Paul's absence; like Paul he is poor judge of mood. Proud of his bargains he reacts amiably to Evelyn's criticism, shadow boxing 'playfully ... near her face' (p. 21). John shows more sympathy for Gordon's illness than Paul. He exploits Paul's appearance to discuss his latest business proposition.

Alone with Paul he denies informing Diana about Evelyn. When Evelyn told him, he was shocked, 'not bitter' (p. 29). Like Paul he seems delighted to see Colin again. He ignores Paul's slight, the carelessly thrown cigar. His failure to light it is comical; the lighter must be another useless bargain. Paul smartly rebukes him for claiming 'We do each other the odd favour' (p. 32) and mentions John's unsaleable cat food. Undeterred John puts forward a new line, literally chasing Paul while outlining the potential profits. He shows some concern for Colin by following him out to the car, but resumes his restless pacing after Colin talks about Carol's death. He manages a 'ghastly smile' (p. 41), when Colin admires his happy marriage.

Consider whether John behaves more humanely than Paul in Act II. John's hurried departure when Colin talks about Carol's death is **ironically** (see Literary Terms) interpreted by Colin as proof that 'John is a very high powered individual – can't sit still always on the move' (p. 46), who will be dominant in his marriage. In fact John's **dramatic monologue** (see Literary Terms), shows that the silent, morose Evelyn is stronger, pervading their entire life with her 'Misery' (p. 61). He is embarrassed by Evelyn's anecdote about the screwdriver and by Diana pouring cream over Paul. When he talks about the safe topic of cars, Evelyn annoys him by carping remarks about the new car carpet. He urges her to 'Lay off' (p. 55): the first time he has stood up for himself.

When Diana breaks down, John helps Marge carry Diana upstairs. He invites Colin to visit his house, although bitterly describing his wife as a 'strong silent woman' (p. 61). He attempts again to interest Paul in a deal and gains a perverse pleasure eavesdropping on Marge and Gordon's telephone argument. For once he makes a perceptive comment, questioning whether Gordon is 'good for' (p. 63) Marge.

He allows Evelyn to decide it is time to leave and stares out the window, relaxed enough to sit down and postpone cutting the new carpet until the next day.

Marge

Marge is a foil to the tactless Evelyn and the only childless woman. She is Diana's trusted friend. Initially Marge seems a comic figure, cooing sentimentally over the baby and demanding admiration for her unsuitable new shoes. She is actually **pathetic**: her maternal instincts have been thwarted and misdirected, caring for her invalid husband.

Marge is generous. Diana says Marge is 'always buying us things' (p. 5). Her life is sad, as Gordon opposes her desire to adopt. She feels so guilty going to the tea party that she telephones him from Diana's house. **Ironically** (see Literary Terms) addressing him with childish endearments, like 'Jumjums' (p. 9), she herself admits 'Honestly, I don't know what I want children for, living with Gordon' (p. 10).

Caring, pathetic and generous
Sympathetic
Tactful and domesticated

Alone with Evelyn, struggling with embarrassment, she asks Evelyn for the truth. Sickened by Evelyn's crude, frank comments on sex, she is very shocked that Evelyn has told John everything, and castigates her as 'heartless, cruel and disgusting' (p. 17). She blames Evelyn for the 'atmosphere between' (p. 18) Paul and Diana.

She is knitting a jumper for Gordon's weak chest, but starts dropping stitches when she senses Diana's anxiety. When Paul criticises Diana, she loyally supports her, 'We can try. It'll only be for an hour' (p. 23) – she reminds Paul that Colin needs to feel 'he's among friends, not enemies' (p. 24). She literally stands between the arguing Paul and Diana until totally diverted by Gordon's telephone call – a comic interlude as she fusses over trivial domestic disasters. Paul selects Marge as the 'calmest' (p. 28) person to answer the door to Colin.

Marge acts as peacemaker.

Off stage she tries to calm Diana, mentioning safe topics when they all reassemble for tea. She reassures Diana when Colin exits. Like Diana she believes deep emotions should be articulated, 'You have to say it' (p. 37). She listens sympathetically to Colin's commentary on his photographs and conceals her tears, blowing her nose at Colin's speech on marriage.

Notice how Marge is excellent in a crisis.

Marge takes over Diana's role of hostess, praising her absent friend as, 'Loyal and trusting' (p. 43). Her memories of the stately home visit are bad: it rained and Gordon got lost. Her pride in her cooking is revealed when Colin comments on Gordon's large size. Sentimentally, she sighs over Colin's and Carol's first kiss and the story of the table napkin. Her remark that 'All men are romantics at heart' (p. 52) is **ironical** (see Literary Terms): Paul immediately shatters this illusion. Typically Marge cleans up the creamy mess.

She immediately takes control of the hysterical Diana: ordering Evelyn to clear up Diana's vomit; instructing John to help her carry Diana upstairs; calming and sedating Diana, while simultaneously dealing with Gordon's complaints on the phone. We pity her when Colin intervenes on the extension, praising her as 'a real treasure' (p. 63). And when Colin advises her to cheer Gordon up, she snaps at Colin for the first time. But she recovers and politely wishes him well, kindly offering to return to help Paul once she's seen to Gordon. Her humane caring words provide an **ironic** (see Literary Terms) ending to the play.

G<small>ORDON</small>
Large and accident-prone
Sickly and selfish

Gordon like Carol is an absent friend, who never appears on stage although he makes his presence felt in three telephone calls to Marge. His ambition was to play County cricket as a left-armed bowler, but he broke his shoulder and became a fire prevention officer instead. He takes out his frustrations on Marge, who ably nurses him through a number of minor illnesses including food poisoning; a bad cough and cold prevent him attending this tea party.

He is the butt of male jokes: Paul cruelly suggests Marge should insure Gordon against illness, while Colin remembers Gordon being sick in the broom cupboard at his farewell party. Colin recalls Gordon 'was famous for his appetite' (p. 49); now he is fat and overweight. Only Diana commiserates with Marge. Gordon is obviously sterile, undergoing fertility tests and refusing to adopt a child. Instead, he acts like a child himself, demanding constant care and sympathy.

When Marge first telephones, he asks for directions to locate the nose drops. He phones Marge back, making her feel guilty that he has clumsily bumped into the furniture, spilling cough mixture over his pyjamas and the bed. The third time he telephones complaining his hot-water bottle has burst. John eavesdrops, describing Gordon as 'a big fat moaner' (p. 62). While he is ranting, Colin fatally intervenes on the line to praise Marge, making matters worse. Gordon's emotional blackmail succeeds; Marge feels she 'can't leave him on his own again when he's ill' (p. 66).

COLIN

Colin acts as a **catalyst** (see Literary Terms), revealing the underlying tensions in the other characters' marriages and their attitudes to bereavement.

He is absent for most of Act I, yet most conversation revolves around the problem of what to say to him. However, **ironically** (see Literary Terms), far from being embarrassed about death, he comes to the tea party primed with snapshots and memories.

Pleased to see his old mates, John and Paul, Colin recalls his absent friend Gordon was sick at his farewell party. Admiring the baby, he reminds John of his ambition to 'get married and have a son' (p. 29). He approves of Paul's success, but believes John possesses a

Cheerful and
idealistic
Romantic
Obtuse and
tactless
'good brain' and that he is 'clever – wonderful with his hands' (p. 46). Colin has a singular talent for misjudging his friends: in fact John is a clumsy, unsuccessful salesman. The embarrassment Colin causes his friends creates humour. He is impervious to the disaster he sets in train: he believes he can 'sum people up pretty quickly' (p. 45), and is 'an expert' (p. 47) on Paul as well as John. He romanticises marriage, attributes Diana's distress to overwork and naïvely believes that praising the tea will rectify the situation.

Consider how
Colin's well-
meant comments
create embarrass-
ment and
laughter.
He nostalgically describes their last abortive outing to a stately home as 'marvellous' (p. 48). The repetition of this word and the other characters' incredulity create **irony** (see Literary Terms). He is constantly cheerful, delighted to have a captive audience for his romantic memories and photos of 'perfect' (p. 40) Carol. We sense that Carol's parents also feel trapped: Colin mentions he often discusses 'old times' and 'out come the old albums' (p. 65). He has pedantically calculated the exact length of his relationship with Carol: 'Fourteen months, twenty-three days' (p. 44), possibly because he works with figures in his steady job at the bank.

Note how Colin
precipitates
Diana's
breakdown.
He relates the story of the table napkin, advising Diana that Paul's gruff exterior hides his 'gentleness' (p. 54). In the ensuing crisis he is horrified and ineffectual. His dense remark, 'There's something very wrong here' (p. 59), raises a laugh. He tactlessly advises Paul to go upstairs to Diana, convinced he has made Paul feel 'brighter' (p. 60). Similarly he dispenses ill-timed advice to the irate Gordon, failing to realise that he has interrupted a private call. His remark, 'Don't want to be in the way' (p. 61), is **dramatically ironic** (see Literary Terms): the characters collapse with exhaustion after he leaves. His insensitive good humour insulates him from reality, making him a dangerous character.

LANGUAGE & STYLE

Ayckbourn adopts a **naturalistic style** of dialogue, which reflects the way his characters speak; there is very little use of **imagery** (see Literary Terms).

GENDER AND LANGUAGE

Note the differences in attitude and in subject matter between the two sexes:

- While the men discuss football, cars and business, Diana and Marge confide their problems to each other. Significantly Paul often interrupts Colin, while Diana and Marge listen carefully, encouraging Colin to speak. Diana tries hard to voice their concern as human beings, 'After all, in this world, we are all to some extent – we're all – what's the word ...?' She breaks off in embarrassment. However, Paul pedantically insists that his word 'Joined' has the same meaning as Diana's word 'Dependent' (p. 36).

Contrast Paul's and Diana's treatment of Colin.

- Sexist language is used by Paul, who patronisingly addresses the women as a 'Mothers' Meeting' (p. 13) and casually walks out – 'I'll leave you ladies to it' (p. 14).
- Evelyn retaliates with the comment 'Hark at Mr Universe.' (p. 13), aptly describing his monstrous egotism.

BABY TALK

Baby talk is used effectively in a number of different ways:

- The maternal Diana compares Evelyn's innocent sleeping baby to chubby angels, 'They look so lovely ... like little cherubims' (p. 1).
- By contrast Evelyn's only endearment is 'little devil, he's really fighting to stay awake' (p. 64).
- **Ironically** (see Literary Terms) Marge describes both the baby and Gordon as 'little': Gordon, ill in bed, is

a 'poor little thing' like 'Little baby Walter' (p. 4).
She later addresses Gordon as 'sweetie' (p. 9),
treating him like a helpless child, murmuring
'rub it better' (p. 10) and 'sticky. You'll have to
wash' (p. 27).

NICKNAMES

Nicknames can be a very effective way of revealing one
character's attitude to another:
- Colin has a talent for recalling embarrassing old
  nicknames. He remembers angular, Marge as 'the
  stick insect' (p. 33), evoking cruel male laughter.
- He tactlessly addresses Gordon by his nickname
  'Jumbo' (p. 63), on the telephone.
- Marge makes Gordon's size more bearable by
  converting the nickname to the diminutive 'JumJums'
  (p. 9).

WITTY IMAGES

Imagery is used sparingly but to great effect:
- Marge laughs when Gordon is compared to a
  'polythene bag full of water' (p. 10), suggesting
  that he is large and flabby! He weighs over sixteen
  stone.
- Evelyn comments **satirically** (see Literary Terms) on
  Paul's infidelities: 'He's halfway through the Yellow
  Pages by now' (p. 18), suggesting that he is
  indiscriminate and promiscuous.
- Evelyn compares sex with sweaty Paul to 'being made
  love to by a sack of clammy cement' (p. 17).

DRAMATIC MONOLOGUES

Ayckbourn gives Diana, Colin and John **dramatic
monologues** (see Literary Terms), long speeches in

which they speak aloud their thoughts, although the
other characters on stage often don't listen or understand what they are saying.

Diana's dramatic monologues (see Literary Terms) reveal her insecurity and self-doubt.

- Diana has two important speeches. At the beginning
  of the play she talks to Evelyn, who ignores her. She
  is 'running herself down', highlighting Paul's good
  qualities 'his amazing energy' and excusing his
  infidelities as she is inadequate 'I don't think I'm
  really enough for him'; then contradicting herself 'But
  he couldn't do without me' (p. 3). Her self-deception
  is **pathetic** (see Literary Terms).

- At the end of the play Diana has a long speech,
  recalling her childish disappointment in a birthday
  present, a red coat she had badly coveted which did
  not suit her. This prefigured her present
  disillusionment with all the feminine
  accomplishments she was brought up to practise:
  'typing and knitting and nursing and having babies'.
  She sacrificed her ambition of a career in the
  Mounted Police, married Paul and had children.
  She is deeply hurt that he won't 'let her keep them'
  (p. 56). Ayckbourn evokes a tragicomic mood in this
  speech.

- Colin's **dramatic monologue**, about Carol's death
  and the other characters' supposedly happy marriages,
  is placed at the end of Act I, where it creates
  devastating **irony** in its **juxtaposition** (see Literary
  Terms) both to the marital arguments preceding
  his arrival and to the impotent, silent reactions of
  the characters. Colin is not 'bitter' that Carol died
  nor does he 'begrudge' (p. 40) his friends their
  happiness.

- John bitterly jokes about his unhappy marriage,
  repeating the word 'miserable' (p. 61) three times to
  describe Evelyn, the baby and his family, not
  expecting anyone to listen: 'Am I keeping you
  awake?' (p. 61).

CLICHÉS AND PLATITUDES

Colin creates verbal humour by either stating the obvious or totally misjudging people.

- Colin was 'over the moon' (p. 49) when Carol kissed him.
- He describes death as 'one of the few things we have all got in common' (p. 40).
- Colin believes John is the 'driver' in his marriage with Evelyn in the 'back seat' (p. 46); in fact Evelyn is dominant.
- His worst *faux pas* is his character portrayal of Paul: 'ashamed of his own nature', covering up his softness altruistically so that he can provide Diana with 'everything a human being could ask for' (p. 54). The audience must laugh very uneasily here, especially after Evelyn suggests that Colin's advice is as hackneyed as articles in a woman's magazine.

PART FOUR

Study skills

How to use quotations

One of the secrets of success in writing essays is the way you use quotations. There are five basic principles:
- Put inverted commas at the beginning and end of the quotation
- Write the quotation exactly as it appears in the original
- Do not use a quotation that repeats what you have just written
- Use the quotation so that it fits into your sentence
- Keep the quotation as short as possible

Quotations should be used to develop the line of thought in your essays.

Your comment should not duplicate what is in your quotation. For example:

> **Marge jokes that Gordon is ill so regularly that she has to buy first aid tins each day like loaves of bread: 'I get through first aid tins like loaves of bread' (p. 10).**

Far more effective is to write:

> **Marge jokes that Gordon's illnesses require daily purchases of medicaments: 'I get through first aid tins like loaves of bread.'**

However, the most sophisticated way of using the writer's words is to embed them into your sentence:

> **Marge jokes that first aid tins for sick Gordon are essential daily purchases 'like loaves of bread'.**

When you use quotations in this way, you are demonstrating the ability to use text as evidence to support your ideas - not simply including words from the original to prove you have read it.

Everyone writes differently. Work through the suggestions given here and adapt the advice to suit your own style and interests. This will improve your essay-writing skills and allow your personal voice to emerge.

The following points indicate in ascending order the skills of essay writing:
- Picking out one or two facts about the story and adding the odd detail
- Writing about the text by retelling the story
- Retelling the story and adding a quotation here and there
- Organising an answer which explains what is happening in the text and giving quotations to support what you write

....

- Writing in such a way as to show that you have thought about the intentions of the writer of the text and that you understand the techniques used
- Writing at some length, giving your viewpoint on the text and commenting by picking out details to support your views
- Looking at the text as a work of art, demonstrating clear critical judgement and explaining to the reader of your essay how the enjoyment of the text is assisted by literary devices, linguistic effects and psychological insights; showing how the text relates to the time when it was written

The dotted line above represents the division between lower- and higher-level grades. Higher-level performance begins when you start to consider your response as a reader of the text. The highest level is reached when you offer an enthusiastic personal response and show how this piece of literature is a product of its time.

Coursework essay

Set aside an hour or so at the start of your work to plan what you have to do.

- List all the points you feel are needed to cover the task. Collect page references of information and quotations that will support what you have to say. A helpful tool is the highlighter pen: this saves painstaking copying and enables you to target precisely what you want to use.
- Focus on what you consider to be the main points of the essay. Try to sum up your argument in a single sentence, which could be the closing sentence of your essay. Depending on the essay title, it could be a statement about a character: Colin acts as a catalyst in the play, exposing the weaknesses in the marriages of his friends; an opinion about setting: all the action on stage takes place in Paul and Diana's living room, which adds to the claustrophobic atmosphere; or a judgement on a theme: Love and marriage is a key theme in the play.
- Make a short essay plan. Use the first paragraph to introduce the argument you wish to make. In the following paragraphs develop this argument with details, examples and other possible points of view. Sum up your argument in the last paragraph. Check you have answered the question.
- Write the essay, remembering all the time the central point you are making.
- On completion, go back over what you have written to eliminate careless errors and improve expression. Read it aloud to yourself, or, if you are feeling more confident, to a relative or friend.

If you can, try to type your essay, using a word processor. This will allow you to correct and improve your writing without spoiling its appearance.

Examination essay

The essay written in an examination often carries more marks than the coursework essay even though it is written under considerable time pressure.

In the revision period build up notes on various aspects of the text you are using. Fortunately, in acquiring this set of York Notes on *Absent Friends*, you have made a prudent beginning! York Notes are set out to give you vital information and help you to construct your personal overview of the text.

Make notes with appropriate quotations about the key issues of the set text. Go into the examination knowing your text and having a clear set of opinions about it.

In most English Literature examinations you can take in copies of your set books. This in an enormous advantage although it may lull you into a false sense of security. Beware! There is simply not enough time in an examination to read the book from scratch.

In the examination

- Read the question paper carefully and remind yourself what you have to do.
- Look at the questions on your set texts to select the one that most interests you and mentally work out the points you wish to stress.
- Remind yourself of the time available and how you are going to use it.
- Briefly map out a short plan in note form that will keep your writing on track and illustrate the key argument you want to make.
- Then set about writing it.
- When you have finished, check through to eliminate errors.

To summarise, these are the keys to success:

- **Know the text**
- **Have a clear understanding of and opinions on the storyline, characters, setting, themes and writer's concerns**
- **Select the right material**
- **Plan and write a clear response, continually bearing the question in mind**

SAMPLE ESSAY PLAN

A typical essay question on *Absent Friends* is followed by a sample essay plan in note form. This does not present the only answer to the question. Try to think of some other ideas of your own, and do not be afraid to exclude some of the following if you feel you have more original ideas. Remember that quotations are essential to prove and illustrate the points you make.

Examine the role of Marge's, and Gordon's telephone conversations in the play. Do you find the calls humorous?

Introduction
There are three telephone calls: the first is made by Marge and the other two by Gordon to induce feelings of guilt: Marge has left him alone to visit their friends. Their function is threefold:

* To reveal the state of their marriage
* To add comedy to the chaos preceding Colin's arrival in Act I and Diana's hysteria in Act II
* To add an additional perspective to the theme of friendship: Gordon is another absent friend

Part 1
Examine Marge's brief call (pp. 9–10), noting down what is revealed about their marriage and Gordon's illness. Do you find the baby talk embarrassing, funny or **pathetic**? Remember Gordon refuses to adopt a child.

Part 2
Briefly set Gordon's phone call in context by outlining why this is a bad time to ring (pp. 24–8). Look at the **juxtaposition** (see Literary Terms) of humour in Gordon's trivial complaints and Marge's baby talk with Diana's, Paul's and Evelyn's simultaneous altercation about adultery. Note the extra sounds adding to the tension.

Part 3
Briefly set Gordon's final call in Act II in context by showing why this is the worst possible time for Marge, who is coping with Diana's breakdown upstairs. Apparently Gordon is ringing to complain about his

hot-water bottle bursting (pp. 62–3), but really to make Marge feel obliged to rush home. Notice the effect of John eavesdropping and Colin intervening on the extension. How does Colin create humour with his advice?

Conclusion   Gordon has succeeded: look at Marge's final speech in the play. He is a domestic tyrant, bullying Marge and using his illness as a weapon.

FURTHER QUESTIONS

Make a plan as shown above and attempt these questions.

1 Show how the use of continuous time and place adds to the claustrophobic atmosphere of the play.
2 Examine two incidents you have found dramatically effective and give reasons for your choice.
3 'The play is a tragicomedy.' To what extent does Ayckbourn successfully mix unhappiness with humour?
4 Ayckbourn has been praised for his 'marked compassion for women'. Do you agree that the female characters are more sympathetically drawn than the male characters?
5 Compare and contrast Marge and Evelyn. Discuss the importance of Evelyn in the play.
6 Do you think Diana has wasted her life 'doing all the wrong things'?
7 How far does Paul fit the stereotype 'male chauvinist pig'?
8 Examine Marge's and Gordon's relationship. Is it mainly humorous or sad?
9 Show how Colin acts as a **catalyst** (see Literary Terms) in the play. Do you think he is a likeable character?

10 Analyse two of Colin's speeches and explain why
    they create painful laughter.
11 Discuss Ayckbourn's presentation of the theme of
    work in the play, contrasting male and female work.
12 Examine the significance of the play's title, *Absent
    Friends*.
13 The mood at the end of the play is predominantly
    pessimistic.' Do you agree?
14 Analyse two dramatic monologues by different
    characters, showing how they are dramatically
    effective.
15 Write a script for *either* the offstage argument
    Diana has with Paul upstairs in Act I *or* the scene in
    the bedroom where Marge and John help Diana in
    Act II. Add director's notes in a commentary,
    explaining the roles of the actors and the methods
    used to create tension.
16 Write the dialogue for two of Gordon's and Marge's
    telephone calls. Add a commentary analysing your
    work.
17 Write an alternative ending or the beginning of a
    further Act imitating Ayckbourn's style. Give
    reasons for the changes you have made.
18 Compare Ayckbourn's treatment of marriage in
    Absent Friends with Mike Leigh's play *Abigail's
    Party*.
19 Compare Ayckbourn's presentation of death with
    Priestley's in *An Inspector Calls*.
20 Compare the theme of male and female work in
    Willy Russell's play *Educating Rita* with the way
    Ayckbourn handles the theme in *Absent Friends*. Do
    you consider Rita to be better equipped for life than
    Diana?

PART FIVE

CULTURAL CONNECTIONS

BROADER PERSPECTIVES

The best way to appreciate Ayckbourn's skill as a dramatist is to see one of his plays. *Absent Friends* was revived by Ayckbourn in Scarborough in 1997 and M. Simkins, formerly an actor at Scarborough, directed the play at Greenwich in London also in 1997. Unfortunately the BBC Television production made in 1985 is not available on video. The popularity of the play is a sign of its success as a comedy of manners, showing the perennial flaws in male and female relationships.

RECENT PLAYS

- In 1998 *Things We Do For Love* was produced in the West End with Jane Asher playing the female lead. The play was originally designed for the smaller conventional auditorium in Scarborough on three levels, depicting the three floors of the house which the unmarried career girl, Barbara, owns. The stage set reflects the play's theme, contrasting the attitudes to love and sex of the inhabitants of each floor, which range from obsessive clothes fetishism to schoolgirl crushes and lust.
- *Comic Potential* was directed by Ayckbourn at Scarborough in 1998. It depicts love between Adam, a human male, and JCF 3133, a robot.

BOOKS

The following books are useful:

I. Watson, *Conversations with Ayckbourn* (Macdonald, 1981); M. Page, *File on Ayckbourn* (Methuen, 1989); M. Billington, *Modern Dramatists, Alan Ayckbourn* (Macmillan, 1990); O. Kerensky, *New British Drama* (Hamish Hamilton, 1977).

bathos/bathetic the use of deflation to create comedy; the sudden descent from elevated to trivial language

black comedy drama in which potentially tragic or unpleasant situations are treated with cynical amusement

catalyst originally a term used in chemistry to describe a substance that increases the rate of chemical reaction without undergoing any change itself. From this it has come to mean, in literary terms, a person or thing that causes change

cliché a boring phrase, made tedious and meaningless by frequent repetition

device a dramatic method or technique

dramatic irony the audience know more than the characters on stage

dramatic monologue a long speech made by one person that is something more than an expression of feeling: the speaker is placed in a situation which is also dramatically realised through what he or she says

Dramatic Unities Greek tragedies concentrated on one complete action or events that took place within a single day and night. Later a single setting was added. In the late sixteenth century scholars came to regard unity of action, time and place as a rule for the proper structure of a play

farce comedy with exaggerated, sometimes improbable, actions from the characters

imagery word pictures to compare two objects

irony the writer says one thing while implying the opposite; for example the well-meant cheerful speeches of Colin have a disastrous effect

juxtaposition placing ideas side by side for emphasis

naturalistic style a style that imitates everyday speech, without artificial figures of speech and without necessarily having a structure of correct grammar or syntax

pathos/pathetic arousing feelings of sorrow and pity

prophetic irony by chance the characters predict the future

satire critical writing employing sarcastic humour to ridicule people, events and ideas

tragic sad or serious event often resulting in disaster or death

tragicomedy a play in which serious and comic scenes are blended

TEST ANSWERS

TEST YOURSELF (Act 1 Part 1 pp. 1–29)

A 1 Diana
2 Marge
3 Paul
4 Evelyn
5 John
6 Gordon
7 Colin
8 John
9 Wayne, the baby
10 Marge

TEST YOURSELF (Act 1 Part 2 pp. 29–41)

A 1 Colin
2 John
3 Diana
4 Paul

5 Colin
6 John
7 John
8 Evelyn
9 Colin
10 Carol

TEST YOURSELF (Act II pp. 42–66)

A 1 Colin
2 Colin
3 Paul
4 Diana
5 Diana
6 John
7 Gordon
8 Paul
9 Gordon

OTHER TITLES

GCSE and equivalent levels (£3.50 each)

Maya Angelou
I Know Why the Caged Bird Sings

Jane Austen
Pride and Prejudice

Alan Ayckbourn
Absent Friends

Elizabeth Barrett Browning
Selected Poems

Robert Bolt
A Man for All Seasons

Harold Brighouse
Hobson's Choice

Charlotte Brontë
Jane Eyre

Emily Brontë
Wuthering Heights

Shelagh Delaney
A Taste of Honey

Charles Dickens
David Copperfield

Charles Dickens
Great Expectations

Charles Dickens
Hard Times

Charles Dickens
Oliver Twist

Roddy Doyle
Paddy Clarke Ha Ha Ha

George Eliot
Silas Marner

George Eliot
The Mill on the Floss

William Golding
Lord of the Flies

Oliver Goldsmith
She Stoops To Conquer

Willis Hall
The Long and the Short and the Tall

Thomas Hardy
Far from the Madding Crowd

Thomas Hardy
The Mayor of Casterbridge

Thomas Hardy
Tess of the d'Urbervilles

Thomas Hardy
The Withered Arm and other Wessex Tales

L.P. Hartley
The Go-Between

Seamus Heaney
Selected Poems

Susan Hill
I'm the King of the Castle

Barry Hines
A Kestrel for a Knave

Louise Lawrence
Children of the Dust

Harper Lee
To Kill a Mockingbird

Laurie Lee
Cider with Rosie

Arthur Miller
The Crucible

Arthur Miller
A View from the Bridge

Robert O'Brien
Z for Zachariah

Frank O'Connor
My Oedipus Complex and other stories

George Orwell
Animal Farm

J.B. Priestley
An Inspector Calls

Willy Russell
Educating Rita

Willy Russell
Our Day Out

J.D. Salinger
The Catcher in the Rye

William Shakespeare
Henry IV Part 1

William Shakespeare
Henry V

William Shakespeare
Julius Caesar

William Shakespeare
Macbeth

William Shakespeare
The Merchant of Venice

William Shakespeare
A Midsummer Night's Dream

William Shakespeare
Much Ado About Nothing

William Shakespeare
Romeo and Juliet

William Shakespeare
The Tempest

William Shakespeare
Twelfth Night

George Bernard Shaw
Pygmalion

Mary Shelley
Frankenstein

R.C. Sherriff
Journey's End

Rukshana Smith
Salt on the snow

John Steinbeck
Of Mice and Men

Robert Louis Stevenson
Dr Jekyll and Mr Hyde

Jonathan Swift
Gulliver's Travels

Robert Swindells
Daz 4 Zoe

Mildred D. Taylor
Roll of Thunder, Hear My Cry

Mark Twain
Huckleberry Finn

James Watson
Talking in Whispers

William Wordsworth
Selected Poems

A Choice of Poets

Mystery Stories of the Nineteenth Century including The Signalman

Nineteenth Century Short Stories

Poetry of the First World War

Six Women Poets

York Notes Advanced (£3.99 each)

Margaret Atwood
The Handmaid's Tale

Jane Austen
Mansfield Park

Jane Austen
Persuasion

Jane Austen
Pride and Prejudice

Alan Bennett
Talking Heads

William Blake
Songs of Innocence and of Experience

Charlotte Brontë
Jane Eyre

Emily Brontë
Wuthering Heights

Geoffrey Chaucer
The Franklin's Tale

Geoffrey Chaucer
General Prologue to the Canterbury Tales

Geoffrey Chaucer
The Wife of Bath's Prologue and Tale

Joseph Conrad
Heart of Darkness

Charles Dickens
Great Expectations

John Donne
Selected Poems

George Eliot
The Mill on the Floss

F. Scott Fitzgerald
The Great Gatsby

E.M. Forster
A Passage to India

Brian Friel
Translations

Thomas Hardy
The Mayor of Casterbridge

Thomas Hardy
Tess of the d'Urbervilles

Seamus Heaney
Selected Poems from Opened Ground

Nathaniel Hawthorne
The Scarlet Letter

James Joyce
Dubliners

John Keats
Selected Poems

Christopher Marlowe
Doctor Faustus

Arthur Miller
Death of a Salesman

Toni Morrison
Beloved

William Shakespeare
Antony and Cleopatra

William Shakespeare
As You Like It

William Shakespeare
Hamlet

William Shakespeare
King Lear

William Shakespeare
Measure for Measure

William Shakespeare
The Merchant of Venice

William Shakespeare
Much Ado About Nothing

William Shakespeare
Othello

William Shakespeare
Romeo and Juliet

William Shakespeare
The Tempest

William Shakespeare
The Winter's Tale

Mary Shelley
Frankenstein

Alice Walker
The Color Purple

Oscar Wilde
The Importance of Being Earnest

Tennessee Williams
A Streetcar Named Desire

John Webster
The Duchess of Malfi

W.B. Yeats
Selected Poems

Chinua Achebe
Things Fall Apart

Edward Albee
Who's Afraid of Virginia Woolf?

Margaret Atwood
Cat's Eye

Jane Austen
Emma

Jane Austen
Northanger Abbey

Jane Austen
Sense and Sensibility

Samuel Beckett
Waiting for Godot

Robert Browning
Selected Poems

Robert Burns
Selected Poems

Angela Carter
Nights at the Circus

Geoffrey Chaucer
The Merchant's Tale

Geoffrey Chaucer
The Miller's Tale

Geoffrey Chaucer
The Nun's Priest's Tale

Samuel Taylor Coleridge
Selected Poems

Daniel Defoe
Moll Flanders

Daniel Defoe
Robinson Crusoe

Charles Dickens
Bleak House

Charles Dickens
Hard Times

Emily Dickinson
Selected Poems

Carol Ann Duffy
Selected Poems

George Eliot
Middlemarch

T.S. Eliot
The Waste Land

T.S. Eliot
Selected Poems

Henry Fielding
Joseph Andrews

E.M. Forster
Howards End

John Fowles
The French Lieutenant's Woman

Robert Frost
Selected Poems

Elizabeth Gaskell
North and South

Stella Gibbons
Cold Comfort Farm

Graham Greene
Brighton Rock

Thomas Hardy
Jude the Obscure

Thomas Hardy
Selected Poems

Joseph Heller
Catch-22

Homer
The Iliad

Homer
The Odyssey

Gerard Manley Hopkins
Selected Poems

Aldous Huxley
Brave New World

Kazuo Ishiguro
The Remains of the Day

Ben Jonson
The Alchemist

Ben Jonson
Volpone

James Joyce
A Portrait of the Artist as a Young Man

Philip Larkin
Selected Poems

D.H. Lawrence
The Rainbow

D.H. Lawrence
Selected Stories

D.H. Lawrence
Sons and Lovers

D.H. Lawrence
Women in Love

John Milton
Paradise Lost Bks I & II

John Milton
Paradise Lost Bks IV & IX

Thomas More
Utopia

Sean O'Casey
Juno and the Paycock

George Orwell
Nineteen Eighty-four

John Osborne
Look Back in Anger

Wilfred Owen
Selected Poems

Sylvia Plath
Selected Poems

Alexander Pope
Rape of the Lock and other poems

Ruth Prawer Jhabvala
Heat and Dust

Jean Rhys
Wide Sargasso Sea

William Shakespeare
As You Like It

William Shakespeare
Coriolanus

William Shakespeare
Henry IV Pt 1

William Shakespeare
Henry V

William Shakespeare
Julius Caesar

William Shakespeare
Macbeth

William Shakespeare
Measure for Measure

William Shakespeare
A Midsummer Night's Dream

William Shakespeare
Richard II

William Shakespeare
Richard III

William Shakespeare
Sonnets

William Shakespeare
The Taming of the Shrew

William Shakespeare
Twelfth Night

William Shakespeare
The Winter's Tale

George Bernard Shaw
Arms and the Man

George Bernard Shaw
Saint Joan

Muriel Spark
The Prime of Miss Jean Brodie

John Steinbeck
The Grapes of Wrath

John Steinbeck
The Pearl

Tom Stoppard
Arcadia

Tom Stoppard
Rosencrantz and Guildenstern are Dead

Jonathan Swift
Gulliver's Travels and The Modest Proposal

Alfred, Lord Tennyson
Selected Poems

W.M. Thackeray
Vanity Fair

Virgil
The Aeneid

Edith Wharton
The Age of Innocence

Tennessee Williams
Cat on a Hot Tin Roof

Tennessee Williams
The Glass Menagerie

Virginia Woolf
Mrs Dalloway

Virginia Woolf
To the Lighthouse

William Wordsworth
Selected Poems

Metaphysical Poets

York Notes – the Ultimate Literature Guides

York Notes are recognised as the best literature study guides.
If you have enjoyed using this book and have found it useful, you
can now order others directly from us – simply follow the ordering
instructions below.

HOW TO ORDER

Decide which title(s) you require and then order in one of the following
ways:

Booksellers
All titles available from good bookstores.

By post
List the title(s) you require in the space provided overleaf,
select your method of payment, complete your name and
address details and return your completed order form and
payment to:
Addison Wesley Longman Ltd
PO BOX 88
Harlow
Essex CM19 5SR

By phone
Call our Customer Information Centre on 01279 623923 to
place your order, quoting mail number: HEYN1.

By fax
Complete the order form overleaf, ensuring you fill in your
name and address details and method of payment, and fax it
to us on 01279 414130.

By e-mail
E-mail your order to us on awlhe.orders@awl.co.uk listing
title(s) and quantity required and providing full name and
address details as requested overleaf. Please quote mail
number: HEYN1. Please do not send credit card details by
e-mail.

York Notes Order Form

Titles required:

Quantity	Title/ISBN	Price

Sub total _____
Please add £2.50 postage & packing _____
(*P & P is free for orders over £50*) _____
Total _____

Mail no: HEYN1

Your Name _____

Your Address _____

_____

Postcode _____ Telephone _____

Method of payment

☐ I enclose a cheque or a P/O for £_____ made payable to Addison Wesley Longman Ltd

☐ Please charge my Visa/Access/AMEX/Diners Club card
Number _____ Expiry Date _____
Signature _____ Date _____

(please ensure that the address given above is the same as for your credit card)

Prices and other details are correct at time of going to press but may change without notice. All orders are subject to status.

☐ *Please tick this box if you would like a complete listing of Longman Study Guides (suitable for GCSE and A-level students)*

York Press

Longman

Addison Wesley Longman